CASE STUDIES IN

CULTURAL ANTHROPOLOGY

GENERAL EDITORS

George and Louise Spindler

STANFORD UNIVERSITY

THE ZINACANTECOS OF MEXICO

A Modern Maya Way of Life

Second Edition

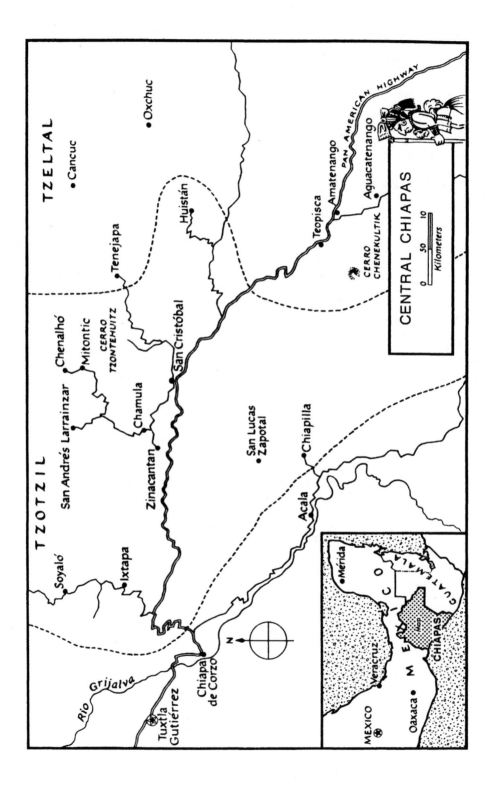

THE ZINACANTECOS
OF MEXICO

A Modern Maya Way of Life

Second Edition

EVON Z. VOGT

Harvard University

WADSWORTH

THOMSON LEARNING

Wadsworth/Thomson Learning
10 Davis Drive
Belmont, CA 94002-3098
USA

For information about our products,
contact us:
Thomson Learning Academic Resource
Center
1-800-423-0563
http://www.wadsworth.com

International Headquarters
Thomson Learning
International Division
290 Harbor Drive, 2ⁿᵈ Floor
Stamford, CT 06902-7477
USA

UK/Europe/Middle East/South Africa
Thomson Learning
Berkshire House
168-173 High Holborn
London WCIV 7AA

Asia
Thomson Learning
60 Albert Street, #15-01
Albert Complex
Singapore 189969

Canada
Nelson Thomson Learning
1120 Birchmount Road
Toronto, Ontario MIK 5G4
Canada
United Kingdom

ISBN 0-030-33344-X

The Adaptable Courseware Program consists of products and additions to existing Wadsworth Group products that are produced from camera-ready copy. Peer review, class testing, and accuracy are primarily the responsibility of the author(s).

To my children,
Skee, Terry, Eric,
and Charlie

Foreword

ABOUT THE SERIES

These case studies in cultural anthropology are designed to bring to students, in beginning and intermediate courses in the social sciences, insights into the richness and complexity of human life as it is lived in different ways and in different places. They are written by men and women who have lived in the societies they write about and who are professionally trained as observers and interpreters of human behavior. The authors are also teachers, and in writing their books they have kept the students who will read them foremost in their minds. It is our belief that when an understanding of ways of life very different from one's own is gained, abstractions and generalizations about social structure, cultural values, subsistence techniques, and the other universal categories of human social behavior become meaningful.

ABOUT THE AUTHOR

Evon Z. Vogt is professor of social anthropology at Harvard University, where he also serves as Curator of Middle American Ethnology and Director of the Harvard Chiapas Project. He holds a Ph.D. in anthropology from the University of Chicago and has taught at Harvard since 1948. He has done field research in the Southwest among the Navaho and Zuni (1947–48, 1949–50, 1951–52) and since 1954 has been making almost yearly field expeditions to Mexico. He is author of *Navaho Veterans*, *Modern Homesteaders*, *Zinacantan*, and *Tortillas for the Gods*. He is coauthor (with Ray Hyman) of *Water Witching: USA*, and coeditor (with W.A. Lessa) of *Reader in Comparative Religion*, (with Ethel M. Albert) of *People of Rimrock*, (with Alberto Ruz) of *Desarrollo Cultural de Los Mayas*, and (with Richard M. Leventhal) of *Prehistoric Settlement Patterns: Essays in Honor of Gordon R. Willey*. He is also the volume editor of Volumes 7 and 8 of the *Handbook of Middle American Indians*. He has served on the Executive Board of the American Anthropological Association, has been a Fellow of the Center for Advanced Study in the Behavioral Sciences, and is a Fellow of the American Academy of Arts and Sciences and a member of the National Academy of Sciences. He has also been decorated by the Republic of Mexico (Knight Commander, Order of the Aztec Eagle).

ABOUT THIS CASE STUDY

The Zinacantecos are Maya tribesmen with a Spanish-Catholic veneer. Their high-backed sandals, worn today for certain ceremonial occasions, are similar to those depicted at archeological sites representing the height of Maya civilization of the ninth century A.D., such as Palenque and Bonampak. The multicolored ribbon streamers on men's hats appear to be a contemporary version of the feathered headdresses worn by the ancient Maya. But the Mayan culture complex revealed in the contemporary behavior of the Zinacantecos goes far beyond limited survivals in costume. Living arrangements, subsistence, social relations, the hierarchical ceremonial structure, and particularly the elaborate conceptual ordering of the universe and other relations between humans and the supernatural all exhibit a basic Mayan character. The Spanish-Catholic elements, particularly in the form of religious figures, religious fiesta days, some priestly functions and ceremonial observances, and in terminology, have synthesized so smoothly with the Mayan complex that the result is a unique, very elaborate, and highly integrated cultural system.

Every step in life for the Zinacantecos is ceremonialized: being pregnant, giving birth, courting, borrowing and repaying money, taking religious office, being cured of illness, and being buried. There are thirty-four religious fiesta days each year, but these account for only a small portion of time spent in ceremonial activity. Readers who live in a culture system low on formal ritual, as in the United States, will gain insight into the ways in which ritual cements social relationships and affirms the interdependence of man and the spiritual forces. This case study is also testimony to the fact that humans create, out of their fantasy, a reality that gives meaning to existence. Individuals in our society, or in any other, may produce in dreams, visions, or drug fugues transient ego-centered realities that deviate in some degree from standard definitions. The Zinacantecos have, as have all culturally distinctive populations in widely varying degrees, created a collective representation of reality that governs the behavior of individuals in every facet of life and that is replicated at all levels of the social structure. The Zinacantecos have gone further in their elaboration of a belief system materially represented in ceremonies, ritual behavior, and daily life than have many other distinctive human communities. This belief system serves as a philosophy, cosmology, theology, code of values, and as a science. It defines, explains, and defends everything about the world. So long as the individual remains within this belief system and so long as the externally imposed conditions of existence do not change too drastically, nothing else need be "known." The Zinacantecos cultural system has endured despite the change from independence before the European invasion to status as a conquered people. It has survived Christian Catholic proselytizing; in fact it has been enriched by it. As an enduring system based upon a traditional codification of phenomena, the Zinacantecos way of believing and behaving is a challenge of the pragmatic empiricism and scientism of Euro-American culture.

The words above were written for the first edition of this case study, published in 1970. They are still applicable today. Though there has been change over the past two decades, there is much that is the same. A new Chapter 9 describes the major features of change and continuity. It ends with this statement, "As Zinacantan approaches the twenty-first century, it presents an overall image of reproductive success, cultural vitality, and a generally successful, if somewhat uneasy, adjustment to the modern world." The chapter fills in the details to support this positive appraisal.

The Zinacanteco population has nearly tripled. Change is apparent in the presence of cars and trucks, electricity, new kinds of houses and clothing, in the economy, and in other areas. But ritual life has exhibited remarkable tenacity and gives meaning to life now as it has for previous generations. Remarkable also is that the Ladinoization so apparent in the 1950's is receding and Indianization is replacing it. In overt manifestations, such as language and costume, and in less visible ways, such as the sense that being Indian is all right, being Mayan in its Zinacanteco form has regained some of its lost status.

Chapter 1 is also entirely new. The Harvard Chiapas Project began in 1957 and has continued to the present. During this long period of fieldwork not only the standby methods of field anthropology, such as participant observation, but also many innovative research techniques were applied. This chapter is a description of the field methods employed in the study of Zinacantecan, and will help newcomers to anthropology to understand that anthropological fieldwork is variegated but rigorous, and adapted to both the purposes of research and the cultural setting in which the research takes place.

In addition to these two new chapters, the text of this case study has been updated with respect to demographic, economic, social, and religious change, as well as change in Zinacanteco material culture. The Introduction has also been expanded and Chapter 9 includes a brief discussion of recent theories about the origins and functions of the cargo system in Mesoamerica.

Ever since its publication in 1970, *The Zinacantecos of Mexico* has been consistently one of the most widely used studies in the CASE STUDIES IN CULTURAL ANTHROPOLOGY series. This new edition should prove useful as well.

George and Louise Spindler
Series Editors
Stanford University

Preface

Field research in Zinacantan was an important part of the Harvard Chiapas Project, which was initiated in 1957. The project has been sponsored by the Center for Behavioral Sciences and Peabody Museum of American Archaeology and Ethnology at Harvard University and by the Instituto Nacional Indigenista in Mexico. The funds for the investigation have been provided by the National Institute of Mental Health of the U.S. Public Health Service (Grants M-1929 and MH-02100), the National Science Foundation (Grants M-1929 and GS-1524), the Carnegie Corporation of New York in the form of a grant (No. 2295) for the Columbia-Cornell-Harvard-Illinois Summer Field Studies Program (which was later supported by the National Science Foundation Grant GY-120), the American Philosophical Society (Grant 2295), and the Harvard Summer School.

In the years since the project began, I have become obligated to a large number of people, both in the United States and in Mexico, who have generously contributed to the success of the research enterprise. In Mexico, I must especially mention Gonzalo Aguirre Beltran and the late Alfonso Caso of the Instituto Nacional Indigenista, Ignacio Bernal and Alfonso Villa Rojas of the Instituto de Investigaciones Antropológicos, the late Alberto Ruz of the Seminario de Cultura Maya, and Leopoldo Velasco Robles and Doña Gertrudis vda. de Blom of San Cristóbal las Casas. In the United States I have profited from the assistance of Gordon R. Willey and my other colleagues at Harvard, as well as those from other universities who have worked in Chiapas, especially Sol Tax, Norman McQuown, A. Kimball Romney, Duane Metzger, Robert Mc. Adams, and Brent Berlin. I am also indebted to Frank Cancian for permission to include his beautiful photographs of Zinacantan, and for providing me with up-to-date demographic data as well as recent data on the cargo system of Zinacantan. I have appreciated the expert editorial work of Sally Price and Linda Blair. Finally, this book would have been impossible without the impressive work of my students and younger colleagues who engaged in field research in Zinacantan and who have contributed so importantly to my understanding of the culture.

Contents

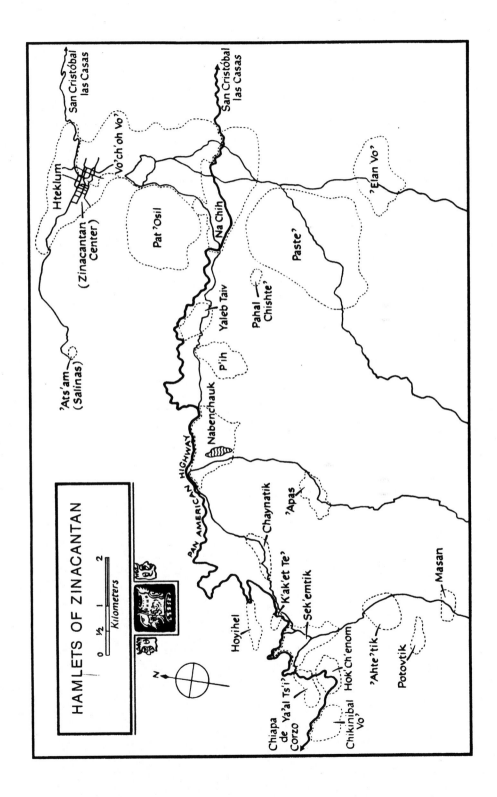

HAMLETS OF ZINACANTAN

Kilometers
0   ½   1   2

N

'Ats'am (Salinas)

San Cristóbal las Casas

Hteklum

(Zinacantan Center)

Vo'ch oh Vo'

Pat 'Osil

San Cristóbal las Casas

Na Chih

'Elan Vo'

Paste'

Yaleb Taiv

Pahal Chishte'

P'ih

Nabenchauk

PAN AMERICAN HIGHWAY

Chaynatik

'Apas

Hoyihel

Kaket Te'

Sek'emtik

Masan

Chiapa de Corzo

Ya'al Tsi' Vo'

Chikinibal Vo'

Hok Ch'enom

'Ahte'tik

Potovtik

Introduction

Zinacantan is one of twenty-one Tzotzil-speaking Indian *municipios* in the Highlands of Chiapas, which are located between the Isthmus of Tehuantepec and the Guatemalan border (see Map 1). Tzotzil is one of the twenty-nine Mayan languages currently spoken by an estimated three million Indians— the descendants of the ancient Maya—who live in Chiapas, the Yucatan Peninsula of Mexico, the Highlands of Guatemala, and Belize.

The Chiapas Highlands rise to over 9000 feet, with fertile upland valleys at 7000 feet, and are composed of rugged limestone and volcanic mountains. Like all of Mexico, Chiapas has marked wet and dry seasons. Almost all the precipitation falls between May and October. While the winters are dry, the heavy summer rains make these Highlands, with a mean annual rainfall of 46 inches, the wettest in Mexico. June and September are the most humid months, with an average monthly precipitation of 10 inches.

On the summit of the Highlands, the climate is cool. During the winter dry season, the days are sunny and warm, and the nights quite cold, with occasional frost in December and January. During the summer rainy season, fog settles in the valleys in the early mornings, the sky is overcast with rain clouds in the afternoons, and it is cool most of the time.

The higher elevations are covered with magnificent stands of pine, interspersed with oak. At lower elevations, stands of oak replace the pines, and the oak in turn gives way to tropical broadleaf forest and savannah in the Lowlands along the banks of the Grijalva River.

The municipio of Zinacantan, covering an area of 117 square kilometers, is located along both sides of the Pan American Highway just west of the city of San Cristobal Las Casas. Zinacantan now has a population of about 20,000 Indians living in a Ceremonial Center and in twenty-six outlying hamlets dispersed throughout the municipio (See Map 2). The Ceremonial Center is situated in a valley at 7000 feet, the hamlets at altitudes ranging from 5000 to 8000 feet.

Zinacantan is located on the western edge of the distribution of the contemporary Maya, whose 29 distinct languages are all differentiated from the Proto-Maya spoken in the ancestral homeland in the Highlands of Guatemala some 4000 years ago (Morley, Brainerd, and Sharer 1983; Vogt 1989).

In addition to language, these contemporary Maya share certain basic patterns of subsistence, social organization, religion, and cosmology. For

1

example, all Mayas today practice swidden agriculture, grow maize, and eat tortillas. They tend to live in patrilocally extended family households. Their religion is a mixture of ancient Mayan and Spanish Catholic patterns. Their cosmology contains an emphasis upon the four corners and the center of the world.

Their cultures vary, of course, because their ancestral ways of life have been adapted for different ecological niches (especially to highland and lowland zones) and they have experienced differing historical contacts with other peoples, such as the PreColumbian Aztecs and the Spanish Conquerors, as well as with the political pressures of the contemporary nation-states and the market forces of the modern world.

The precise prehistoric origins of the contemporary Tzotzil are only partially understood, but inferences based upon archaeological and linguistic research indicate that their ancient Maya ancestors first lived in the highlands of Northwestern Guatemala and later moved to the lowlands along both sides of the Usumacinta River. Here they participated in the remarkable growth of Classic Maya civilization (A.D. 300 to A.D. 900) which built the famous sites of Tikal, Uaxactun, Palenque, Yaxchilan, Bonampak, and others. By about A.D. 200 the ancestors of the Tzotzil, who spoke Tzeltalan, began moving into the Chiapas Highlands where by A.D. 600 they split into the Tzeltal, located to the East, and the Tzotzil, located to the West (See Map 1; Adams 1961; Vogt and Ruz 1964; McVicker 1974; Kaufman 1976).

Aztec merchants from their capital at Tenochtitlan (now Mexico City) reached the Highlands of Chiapas in the fifteenth century and traded for amber, quetzal feathers, and skins. Although they did not conquer the Tzotzil and Tzeltal region as a whole, they did establish a garrison in Zinacantan for a short period to facilitate trading activities (Adams 1961).

It was here in the Chiapas Highlands that the Spanish Conquerors found the Tzotzil and Tzeltal, conquered them in 1528, and established the city of San Cristobal Las Casas, which still serves today as the principal market town and political center for the Highlands. This old colonial city also served as the capital of Chiapas until 1891 when the capital was moved to the newer, more progressive town of Tuxtla Gutierrez in the lowlands, some 45 miles to the west. While the population of San Cristobal has grown to 100,000, it has been outstripped by Tuxtla Gutierrez, which now boasts a burgeoning population of over 800,000.

The descendants of the Spanish conquerors interbred with Indians over the centuries, and became the local Ladinos, who speak Spanish, live mainly in towns and cities, control the economic and political system of Chiapas, are strong Catholics, and consider themselves citizens of the Republic of Mexico. The Indians, on the other hand, speak Tzotzil and Tzeltal, live mainly in small scattered hamlets, are only nominally Catholics, and consider themselves primarily members of their own tribal groups. Each tribal group lives in a single municipio, speaks a unique language, and dresses in distinctive clothes (see Colby 1966).

During the long colonial period the Ladinos established coffee and sugar *fincas* and cattle ranches on the flanks of the highlands and in the lowland valleys. The Indians, first controlled and required to furnish labor under the *encomienda* system by which the Spanish Crown granted the Conquerors' rights to this labor taxation from specified Indian communities, later became peons in great numbers under a system of debt-peonage on large fincas and ranches. The result was a great loss of Indian ancestral lands as well as economic and political control to Ladino landlords and merchants living in the Highland Chiapas towns.

It is not surprising that the Tzotzil participated in two major Indian rebellions against Spanish rule. The "Tzeltal Revolt" of 1712 started in the Tzeltal municipio of Cancuc, but spread rapidly to the Tzotzil area. The "Cuzcat Rebellion" (named after the leader, Pedro Diaz Cuzcat) was initiated in Chamula in 1869, and soon attracted a large following of armed Indians who attacked San Cristobal Las Casas and were repelled only by the arrival of Mexican army troops (Vogt 1969).

The Tzotzil did not begin to recover their ancestral lands until well after the Mexican Revolution of 1910 to 1920. Indeed, it was not until the presidency of Lázaro Cárdenas in 1940 that Zinacantan received its first *ejido* under the land reform system that followed the Revolution.

By 1950 the Pan American Highway had been paved into San Cristobal Las Casas and the Zinacantecos began to ride trucks and busses into market and become even more integrated into the market system of the modern world. For not only did the completion of the highway vastly improve the transportation network for the Zinacantecos, but the highway also greatly aided Zinacanteco merchants who had long been involved in the salt trade and in the sale of surplus maize. It also stimulated the development of new industries, such as the flower industry, for now goods produced in highland hamlets could be trucked to Tuxtla Gutierrez for sale in that large market.

Nineteen fifty also marked the arrival of the *Instituto Nacional Indigenista* (National Indian Institute) in San Cristobal, with its ambitious program to aid the Tzotzil and Tzeltal in improving their life on many fronts: health, education, agriculture, etc. This agency was to be the first of many Mexican governmental programs to assist the Indians of Highland Chiapas in their adjustment to the rapidly developing and changing world of the late twentieth century (see Chapter 9).

1/Field Research
in Zinacantan

My field research in Zinacantan began in 1957, when I initiated the "Harvard Chiapas Project." Headquarters have been maintained continuously since then in the Ladino market town of San Cristobal Las Casas, where we can conduct private interviews and offer hospitality to Zinacanteco informants. Over the past 32 years, my students and I have undertaken fieldwork in the ceremonial center of Zinacantan and in almost all of its 26 hamlets (see Vogt 1969; 1976; 1978). From the beginning we have stressed utilizing the native Indian language in our research, living with Zinacanteco families, working with them in their cornfields, and attending their ceremonies. This participant observation has not been easy, especially on occasions when the ethnographer is confronted with a drinking ritual and expected to consume strong rum liquor at 5 A.M., but the combination of interviewing and observation is still the only reliable way to ethnographic truth. It is genuine tribute both to my students and to the Zinacantecos who have accepted us so gracefully in their homes that we have enjoyed a rich and rewarding experience in investigating and recording this colorful culture for the first time in history. But how did we begin to develop rapport with this remote society? What field methods have we used over the past 32 years? What problems did we encounter and how did we solve them?

THE EARLY BEGINNINGS

When I initiated my research in Zinacantan in the summer of 1957, I was the first ethnographer to undertake sustained field work in this contemporary Mayan society. A small field party of anthropology students from Mexico's National School of Anthropology had engaged in some six weeks of research in Zinacantan Center in the winter of 1942–43 under the direction of Professor Sol Tax of the University of Chicago. But by 1957 this early and brief contact with the anthropological world had almost faded completely from Zinacanteco memories, and I had to begin anew to develop rapport with the people of Zinacantan.

Anthropologists have discovered that upon arrival in an alien society they must work immediately on three matters. They must set about learning the native language as well as enough of everyday customs to shelter and provision themselves and begin the long process of attaining some level of acceptance. They must begin to develop a "role"—that is, a name and a reason for being an intruder that will somehow be meaningful to the people being studied, who clearly will never have heard of anthropology, nor have been introduced to the preposterous idea that it is worth anyone's time to study the customs of another community. Finally, they must also be able to contribute something practical to the people whose time and energies are being absorbed in the anthropological investigation.

My research operations began in early August, 1957, when a graduate student, Frank C. Miller, and I picked up a project Land-Rover in Tuxtla Gutierrez, the state capital of Chiapas. By Landrover, on horseback, and on foot, Miller and I undertook a month-long reconnaissance of the Tzotzil area in order to select sites for field research. This was one of my most difficult months of field experience since we were complete strangers and had so little comprehension of the customs, especially the meanings of the aggressive acts by intoxicated residents of various field sites we visited. More than once we were startled by and uncertain how to handle drunks who babbled incoherently and pushed aggressively against our Landrover as it paused on the back-country roads. By the end of the month, we had learned a great deal about handling these and other situations, and I decided to work in a hamlet of Zinacantan while Miller settled in a hamlet of the neighboring municipio of Huistan.

Aside from two brief articles by a missionary-linguist (Weathers, 1947; 1950), the Tzotzil spoken by the Zinacantecos was an unstudied and unwritten language. Fortunately, many of the Zinacanteco men had learned Spanish (most women were monolingual in Tzotzil) from their limited schooling and from their working and marketing experiences in the Mexican communities of Chiapas. Since I was fluent in Spanish, I could at least begin by having conversations with the bilingual Zinacanteco men and enlist their assistance in learning Tzotzil. Unlike Navaho, a tonal language with a very complex grammatical structure with which I had worked previously in my Southwestern research, Tzotzil proved to be a less than difficult language. An anthropologist with moderate gifts for learning languages can, I estimate, attain a reasonable fluency in Tzotzil by working full-time on the task for six months.

After the 1957 season in Zinacantan, I returned in 1958 with two graduate students, B.N. ("Nick") and Lore M. Colby, who remained in the field for a year. Since Lore Colby was a linguist, she made the first systematic study of Tzotzil grammar and compiled an elementary field dictionary. With her return to Cambridge, we initiated the first informal course in spoken Tzotzil, with Lore Colby serving as the teacher. For the ensuing 20 years, the course in Tzotzil was offered informally almost every spring term at Harvard, and we developed three methods that enormously enhanced the rate at which new students learned Tzotzil before they entered the field for the first time. By mutual agreement, the member of the project who knew Tzotzil best was appointed as the teacher, regardless of age or rank. Some years the teacher was an undergraduate, while I was one of the students. We found this was by all odds the most efficient way to teach the language. Zinacanteco informants were also persuaded to spend six weeks to two months at Harvard each spring to be native speakers in residence for the Tzotzil course and available for pre-field interviewing. These informants, with the skilled help of George A. Collier and John B. Haviland, produced Tzotzil language tapes that were improved each season and kept on file for the students' use in the language laboratories. The most difficult part of this process was arranging the papers and transportation to the United States for the Zinacanteco informants—a procedure that always involved some member of the project traveling to Chiapas, supervising the preparation of the papers (temporary passport, military service card, etc.), then running the gauntlet at the United States Embassy in Mexico for the visa, and another gauntlet at immigration and customs upon arrival in the U.S. The embassy and immigration officials always began by assuming we were trying to import domestic servants! Further, since the informants spoke no English and were unaccustomed to the rigors of life in a city, especially one as cold as Cambridge, Massachusetts, we always arranged to house and feed the informants in one of our own homes. Some member of the project then accompanied the informant back to Chiapas to make certain he did not get lost along the way and/or fail to get through all the immigration and custom checks. But it was all more than worth the time, the expense, and the effort because it was enormously stimulating for the students learning Tzotzil and collecting data for field projects they were planning for the subsequent summer season.

Along with the language, the field ethnographer also needs to learn essential everyday etiquette and anticipated responses to everyday encounters. For example, in Tzotzil, one never says "Good Morning," "Good Afternoon," or "Good Evening," nor anything like "Hello" or "Hi." Rather, when people meet on a trail, the greeting is a very matter-of-fact, "I am passing, Sir," and the response, "Go ahead and pass." Approaching a Zinacanteco house, one never knocks on the door nor even comes close to the door before saying loudly, from *outside* the patio gate, "Are you there, Madam?" (assuming that although the man of the house may be away, the woman of the house is always at home by the hearth). The response is, "I am here"; then one may ask if her husband is there. The etiquette for drinking together or sharing ceremonial meals (see Chapter 8) is complicated and adds up to a lengthy set of rules that would make a respectable chapter in a Zinacanteco version of Emily Post's *Etiquette*.

In developing an understandable role in an alien society, a recognizable name is an essential part of the anthropologist's identity. In my previous field work among the Navaho, my identity was quickly established by my Navaho name. My father, who owned a sheep and cattle ranch that bordered on a part of the Navaho Reservation in western New Mexico, became quite portly in his later years and acquired the Navaho name of "Pesoteaje" ("the little pig"). And I naturally became known as "Pesoteaje Biye" ("the son of the little pig") in the Navaho communities. But here among the Zinacantecos it was obvious from the first season of 1957 that the handle of "Evon Z. Vogt" or "Professor Vogt" was making me more alien than the average stranger with a more pronounceable name. In the summer of 1958 it was the University of Chicago linguist, Norman MacQuown, who made the felicitous suggestion that "Evon" was probably some eccentric family version of "Evan," which in turn was related to "John." "John" translates into "Juan" in Spanish and into "Shun" in Tzotzil, and I could become "Don Juan" in Spanish, or "Totik Shun" ("Sir John") in Tzotzil. With advancing years, the "Totik Shun" became "Mol Shun" ("Old Man John"), a name of greater respect. Similarly, "Vogt" was usually pronounced "Vo' " (the Tzotzil word for water), and my place of origin, "Boston," as "Posh Ton," literally "Rum Liquor Rock." So I became "Mol Shun Vo' " and came from "Posh Ton"—"Old Man John Water from Liquor Rock"—and all was finally understandable to the Zinacantecos!

But what was I really doing spending my time asking impertinent questions about Zinacanteco words and customs? To the more educated and literate Zinacantecos, I simply described myself as a "professor" or "anthropologist"—both roles being somewhat known to the Indians because there were Mexican professors and occasional anthropologists working for the National Indian Institute out of San Cristobal. To the less educated and less sophisticated villagers, the ultimate justification for my presence was that my "patrón" (boss) was named Presidente Derek Bok (of Harvard University) and that he had ordered me to come to Zinacantan and study its customs. Don't ask me why; an order is an order. This seemed to work—as it had for Ben and Lois Paul years before in their field work in the Guatemalan Mayan community of San Pedro La Laguna on Lake Atitlán. As my acquaintanceship grew with the Zinacantecos, and theirs with our work, I always explained in more detail the importance of knowledge about other people's customs and shared with them descriptions of our own peculiar customs—a subject they found fascinating.

Finally, what could I do for the people in practical terms to reimburse them for the time and energy they spent answering my endless questions? At the outset, I discovered the most appreciated service I could provide was rides for people and their goods, especially sacks of maize, to the market in San Cristobal. In 1957, most Zinacantecos walked to market, leaving home at sunrise to reach San Cristobal after a two or three hour journey. To be able to ride in the project Land-Rover and transport their maize, chickens, and eggs for sale in less than one-fourth the usual time was enormously appreciated.

As I began more systematic interviewing, I started to reimburse the Zinacantecos, on the basis of the average daily wage, for their time. Since I was keeping them from working in the fields or engaging in other productive work, it made sense to pay them a daily wage. Thus I became an employer, with all the advantages and disadvantages such a role implies. One advantage was obvious—being able to ask an informant to come to field headquarters in San Cristobal and sit down for a full day to answer my questions. However, the disadvantages also became apparent as I was quickly made aware of the fact that employers are expected to loan money to employees when the maize supply runs short, or when a member of a family is ill and needs to have an expensive curing ceremony performed.

In perspective I shall never forget my first two seasons in the Zinacanteco hamlet of Paste'. Each day I would drive out to the hamlet from headquarters in San Cristobal. I discovered that the teachers in the local school would visit with me, but as I drove along the hamlet roads, not only the people, but also the dogs and sheep, would run to hide in the cornfields at my approach. If accompanied by my wife and children, we would stop for a picnic lunch at the edge of the road, and finally people would emerge from the cornfields, full of curiosity, to engage us in conversation with their halting Spanish and my even more halting Tzotzil. After a few weeks, we were providing transport for people, maize, and chickens to the market, and our Land-Rover resembled scenes from *Teahouse of the August Moon*. Many of the Zinacantecos we transported had never been in a motor vehicle previously; they would become dizzy and ask me to stop, at speeds exceeding five miles an hour. Since they had never sat on a bench or chair before, the women preferred to kneel on the floor (as they do by the fire in their houses when they are grinding maize or cooking food) in the back of the Land-Rover.

By the third season in 1959, using funds that we provided, the National Indian Institute had completed a field house for us in the hamlet of Paste'. It was a small, three-room structure, next to the school house. I moved in, accompanied by my wife, four children, a graduate student, and a Zinacanteco informant from the ceremonial center. The quarters were tight, but we were at last installed in a hamlet, and we were next door neighbors of the Cultural Promoter (as the Indian Institute teachers were called), who proved to be the dominant member of the *ejido* (land reform) committee and hence one of the most important political leaders in all Zinacantan.

Our field house had to be built next to the government school since land in Zinacantan is inalienable in the sense that selling a parcel to an outsider is unthinkable. The Mexican government had already established the school on a piece of land contributed by the community, and hence our house became a kind of appendage of the school. This location proved to be fruitful for getting well acquainted with the Cultural Promoter, who was to become one of my principal informants. I also became well acquainted with the Secretary of the School Committee, whose daily task it was to make certain that the children came to school and to stand guard over the chickens and pigs of the Cultural Promoter when he went home to visit his family in Zinacantan Center. And we certainly became well acquainted with the school children—all still mainly boys in those days (the girls were not sent to school in any number until years later)—who would begin peering in our windows shortly after sunrise since they arose early and had nothing to do but play marbles in the schoolyard until school began at 8 a.m. But our knowledge of Zinacanteco social life was limited since it is not customary just to go visiting in Zinacantan culture. One must have a reason for going to another household: to borrow an axe, buy a chicken, or engage the services of a shaman. So we saw little of the more intimate social life of the community, and while we heard shamans performing curing ceremonies in nearby houses, we were not invited. Indeed, it was not until my fourth season of field work in the spring of 1960 that I finally managed to be invited to attend the ceremonies for the lineages and waterholes, and not until the fifth season that I was invited to attend a curing ceremony in the privacy of a home. These invitations came from the former Secretary of the School Committee, whom I came to know in the summer of 1959. By 1960 he had completed his cycle of dreams, had emerged as one of the shamans of the hamlet, and invited me to attend the ceremonies. In the spring of 1960 I had also managed to arrange to eat my meals with a Zinacanteco family since I was alone in the field, and I explained that without my wife there was nobody to cook my tortillas. The flow of conversation and the observations of family life during meals added immeasurably to my control of the language and to my knowledge of Zinacanteco customs. This early experience of living in the field house in a hamlet led to a fundamental decision concerning field strategy during the later years of the project. I decided it was much more productive to headquarter in San Cristobal where we could interview informants away from the distractions of ordinary Zinacanteco family life—the barking dogs and crying babies, and all members of the family listening in on the interview—and also offer hospitality when Zinacantecos visited us. Then when we went to the villages we arranged to live in Zinacanteco houses, sleeping on the floor as they did, sharing their meals, participating in curing ceremonies as they occurred, etc. After several days to two weeks with a family, the field worker would return to field headquarters in San Cristobal to write up field notes and do some formal interviewing, and then return to the field again. This alternating between living at field headquarters and living directly with Indian families gave us a much deeper view than we could ever have obtained by living beside them as a neighbor, but essentially apart from Zinacantecos, as we did in our own field house in Paste'. The Paste' field house was later given to the community and is now utilized as housing for additional schoolteachers.

THE TRADITIONAL FIELD METHODS:
PARTICIPANT OBSERVATION AND FORMAL INTERVIEWING

The pattern of alternation between field headquarters in San Cristobal and stays of several days to two weeks in the field, living directly with Indian families in Zinacantan Center and various hamlets, permitted us to utilize very productively the two time-honored field methods of ethnographers: participant observation and formal interviewing.

The placing of observers in Zinacanteco houses was a difficult process, especially in the early years when we were still learning the customs. The first overnight stays were arranged with our close informants, especially with the family of a Zinacanteco who had been working with the National Indian Institute puppet show and whom we employed as an informant. Later we were able to place students in many different households in several hamlets by following a procedure the Zinacantecos used themselves in asking for a favor (e.g., a loan of money). We would accompany our request with a liter of rum liquor, assure the family that the student liked beans and tortillas and spoke Tzotzil, and offer to pay a modest daily fee to cover the cost of the meals. Only two concessions were made to add to the health and comfort of the ethnographer living in: a canteen of purified water to drink and a sleeping bag to keep warm during cold nights in the Chiapas mountains. Otherwise we lived as the Indians lived, and participated as fully as possible in the flow of life. Our female students learned to make tortillas, weave, and carry wood and water on tumplines; our male students learned to plant and hoe corn, tend mules, and, if musically talented, play the native musical instruments. We also made an effort to place students in households that would afford maximal information for their particular projects. For example, if a student were studying curing ceremonies, we would place that person in the household of a shaman. On the other hand, if the focus were studying birth, we would place the student in the house of a midwife. I also encouraged our ethnographers to wear appropriate Zinacanteco clothing—a fact that was appreciated by the Indians since they had an opportunity to sell some of the products of their weaving to us. Symbolically, they liked the idea of our wearing their clothing instead of appearing in the villages dressed as Ladinos or other outsiders. We found it was best, however, to wear the clothing after one learned enough Tzotzil to carry on graceful conversations. The two processes of learning the language and dressing as Zinacantecos appropriately went together.

Anthropologists often make a distinction between formal and informal interviews. In the informal interviews the ethnographer does not take notes or record on a tape recorder, but instead chats informally with an informant while sitting around a fire in a house, walking on a mountain trail, or giving an informant a ride in a jeep. We, of course, made use of the informal interviewing when the opportunities presented themselves, but we came to depend more upon day-long formal interviewing at field headquarters in San Cristobal. For our field headquarters, we managed to rent a rustic, old ranch on the outskirts of San Cristobal. The four adobe buildings on what came to be called the "Rancho Harvard" provided housing for staff, rooms for field conferences and parties, and a set of four offices with fireplaces for the quiet space needed to write up field notes on participant observations and informal interviews and to engage informants in formal interviewing. If the student was nearly fluent in Tzotzil, the interview was all in Tzotzil and usually recorded for later transcription. More often the student used a combination of Tzotzil and Spanish, but always attempted to pose the questions in Tzotzil so there would be uniformity in the eliciting from one informant to the next. Formal interviews were often recorded directly on the typewriter; now, of course, they are recorded on portable computers.

A productive combination of interviewing and participant observation can be illustrated by the approach I used in studying the rituals of Zinacantan. I would interview a shaman in advance of a curing ceremony, asking him to tell me in detail what he would do during the ceremony. Then I would participate in the ceremony—some were brief, but some lasted up to 36 hours without a break—and write up my field notes on the event. Afterwards, I would interview the shaman again about what I actually observed, asking especially about what episodes he might have omitted in the first interview, or about departures from the procedure he had outlined. I also developed a special method of interviewing by accompanying the shaman into the woods to collect all the plants needed for a ceremony. We would then bring the plants back to field headquarters, and I would ask him to teach me how to arrange and manipulate the plants for a particular ceremony. Not only did I learn a great deal by manipulating the paraphernalia, but also in the process of gathering the plants and teaching me how to manipulate them, the shaman himself would remember other details to tell me about. The very feel and smell and colors of the sacred plants seemed to set up a very productive eliciting situation.

TEACHING ZINACANTECOS TO READ, WRITE, AND TYPE IN TZOTZIL

At the beginning of the project I discovered that a few Zinacantecos could read and write Spanish, which they had learned in school, but none were literate in Tzotzil. As soon as we had made enough progress in describing Tzotzil, we devised an appropriate alphabet and began teaching a few selected informants to read and write in Tzotzil. This process proved to be a great advantage for them and was also useful for our research since we could ask them to write texts with interlinear translations in Spanish about certain domains of Zinacanteco life (farming, sheep raising, house-building, curing ceremonies, myths, etc.). The next step was to teach a number of informants to touch-type and provide them with portable typewriters. Now the texts could be written with greater ease, and transcriptions from tapes recorded in Tzotzil could be made with the interlinear translations in Spanish. The selected informants were very adept at typing, and even learned to add appropriate footnotes to the texts explaining difficulties in translation. Some of our informants began to be hired to type official papers of various kinds by other Zinacantecos, so that there was high motivation to perfect typing skills, which could be transferred later to portable computers when they were added to our research technology.

Now we were in a position to generate much additional information about the culture because informants could be employed by the day or by the page to type up information on the annual round of activities and send us copies through the mail.

INNOVATIVE FIELD METHODS

In addition to the more traditional methods of anthropological field work, the Harvard Chiapas Project stressed from the outset the development of innovative field methods tailored to the particular research problems of individual anthropologists.

For example, Robert M. Laughlin, who began his field research in Zinacantan in 1959, pioneered a variety of methods as he spent some 12 years compiling his Tzotzil dictionary. He brought informants to Washington and to Santa Fe, New Mexico, for some months to work intensively on the dictionary; he used the technique of "creating" words by running the alphabet through the computer (to see if new combinations of letters reminded the informants of Tzotzil words that had not yet been recorded); with the assistance and encouragement of John Haviland, he had his dictionary computerized. The result is the most complete American Indian language dictionary ever to have been published, appropriately entitled *The Great Dictionary of San Lorenzo Zinacantan*, with more than 35,000 words.

The Cancians, who began field research in Zinacantan in 1960, were also pioneers in innovative methods. Frank Cancian, who specialized in the economics of maize-farming and cargoholding, trained key informants to administer questionnaires in Tzotzil, and was able to obtain almost total samples of household heads in two large hamlets, thereby giving us unprecedented and detailed economic information (1972). Francesca M. Cancian (1964) successfully adapted Robert F. Bales' laboratory techniques for the study of small-group interaction and for scoring the interactions in a sample of ten Zinacanteco households over a 24-hour period. Victoria R. Bricker, in her field study (1973) of the patterns of ritual humor, utilized the tape recorder to record the intricate dialogues carried on during ceremonial clowning. Jane Collier's study (1973) of Zinacanteco law is based not only upon field observations but also on 287 law cases collected by interviewing informants and studying over 15 texts in Tzotzil written by literate Zinacantecos.

For some types of problems, we discovered it was useful to use panels of informants. One example is Carolyn Pope Edwards' study (1969) of Zinacanteco funerals and cemeteries. Utilizing a photograph of the cemetery of one of the hamlets (taken from the top of a nearby mountain ridge), she hoped to elicit from informants the social structure of the cemetery—i.e., who was buried where. The women, who offer candles for dead ancestors each Sunday in the cemeteries, were reluctant to be interviewed. Any given man only knew where his own immediate ancestors were buried. At the suggestion of a key informant, the solution proved to be a panel of 12 men who sat around a long table at field headquarters, looked at the photograph together, and provided complete information on the whole cemetery in a single day of interviewing (Vogt 1978).

Another fruitful use of informants was employed by George Collier and John Haviland, who collected during the summer of 1970 a "Who's Who in Zinacantan." Collier was interested in studying hamlet political structure;

Haviland was interested in the patterns of gossip. Haviland (1977: 13–14) describes the methods used:

> We reasoned that panels of Zinacantecos, selected to be representative and knowledgeable, could produce lists of the well-known people in each hamlet and then supplement these lists with basic identifying information about each person. We found that it was indeed possible to elicit lists of names for each hamlet. The work had two stages. First our panels (of three to five Zinacanteco men) would respond to the question. . . . 'who is best known in each of the hamlets?' When we had exhausted this question, we asked the panel to name people from the hamlet who fell into various categories (e.g., curers, moneylenders) . . . For each name we elicited a cargo history, a record in civil office, age and some rudimentary genealogical information, and we noted short descriptions which occurred while the men on the panel tried to identify the individuals among themselves. We realized that we had managed to capture the skeletal forms of reputations—that we were dealing with incipient gossip, as the men on the panel discussed each man at length, argued over his past performance and joked about his nickname.
>
> The format of the Who's Who eliciting sessions was amenable to gossip as well as to the census-taking we were doing. Therefore, I used the same panel of Zinacantecos to generate stories of the people on the Who's Who lists for three hamlets. The stories were tape-recorded and either edited or fully transcribed in Tzotzil. This was by far the richest source for gossip: I recorded and transcribed more than forty hours of such gossip sessions, replete with wild laughter, joking and mocking as the panel considered the reputations and exploits of Who's Who notables. Losing its initial inhibition, the panel gradually warmed up to the task. Professor Collier and I frequently withdrew from the conversation completely and let the men talk naturally. Conversations continued long after we had left the workroom and turned off the tape recorder.

In 1963, in collaboration with Professors Norman A. MacQuown and A. Kimball Romney, I received a National Science Foundation grant to obtain aerial photographic coverage of the Highlands of Chiapas. The aerial photographs of three kinds—cartographic, high acuity panoramic, and low level obliques—were taken in 1964 by the Companía Mexicana de Aerofotos, S. A., and the Itek Corporation of Palo Alto, California. We later established an aerial photo laboratory at Harvard with a Reader-Printer and zoom stereoscope for viewing and working with photographs, and we produced a basic file of photomosaics and maps for the study of settlement patterns, communications networks, topography, and land use in the Tzotzil and Tzeltal area of the Chiapas Highlands. Each new student who was selected to work in Zinacantan was introduced to the aerial photo laboratory and was able to study and map the specific areas in which he or she would be working during the forthcoming field season, so that aerial photos became useful for almost every field project.

In addition, there were many projects which made very special use of the aerial photographs. George Collier used the aerial photos to make an exhaustive study of demography and land tenure patterns in a hamlet in which questions of land ownership were too delicate to broach when working in the field (1975). Collier also developed a computer program that constructed genealogies on print-out sheets and then located the lineages on computer maps derived from aerial photos. Richard Price developed a method of utilizing aerial photos to study the fallow cycles of Zinacanteco swidden agriculture, and estimated that the work he accomplished in four weeks by using the aerial photography would have taken six months by traditional ground survey methods. Gary Gossen developed ways of utilizing aerial photographs to study world views by eliciting systematic information from informants about sacred geography. Linnea H. Wren made new discoveries about the forking trail patterns of Zinacanteco hamlets that are laid out in a completely different manner from the grid patterns found in Ladino cities in Chiapas (for details, see Vogt 1974).

LONG-TERM FIELD RESEARCH

Perhaps the most distinctive feature of the field research in Zinacantan is the relatively long time-period over which I have had the culture under almost continuous observation (Vogt 1979). From 1957 through 1989, a period of thirty-two years, we have had field observers working in Zinacantan for at least part of each year. The implications of this long-term research are profound. Rapport can develop at a level that is rare in the shorter term field projects, especially those that last only a year or two. After a time in longer term projects, the anthropologists are expected to arrive each year, like the summer rains.

And, while they may not always do all the Zinacantecos expect or hope they will do (such as offering more employment and more loans), they always employ some informants each season; they continue to teach Zinacantecos to type or write in their own Tzotzil language; and they help to increase the pride the Zinacantecos have in their own identity and in their own customs. Quite unlike the local missionaries and government officials, many of whom denigrate native customs, the anthropological presence helps to promote a new self-consciousness, a new self-respect on the part of the Zinacantecos. And the anthropologists can begin to work immediately without waiting long periods for sufficient rapport to develop to permit field observations and interviews. There can also be a sharing of an enormous corpus of data, as each field worker contributes a copy of his field notes to the central archives as they have over the years. Further, each field-worker normally circulates manuscripts to other members of the project for comment and criticism in advance of publication. While I sometimes find it maddening to have to rewrite an article or a book three or four times in response to the sharp comments from my colleagues and former students, I am convinced the final products are better for it, both ethnographically and analytically.

2/The Zinacanteco Universe

The Zinacanteco Indians of Highland Chiapas have drawn on their prehistoric past, their four centuries under Spanish conquerors, and their current confrontation with the modern world in fashioning their present way of life. The unique culture they have developed helps them both in understanding and coping with their particular environment and in carrying forward a vital and meaningful way of life.

While the elements of this way of life are all intimately interrelated, I have quite arbitrarily divided them into a series of chapters—beliefs about the universe, the organization into a ceremonial center and outlying hamlets, social life, economics, the life cycle, and rituals. While these chapters dissect and analyze the culture into some of its more important components, I hope the reader will be able to synthesize the diverse elements, superimposing one description onto another to form a picture of a highly integrated system, and thus to approach more nearly the Zinacanteco view of their own way of life.

THE QUADRILATERAL COSMOS

The rugged limestone and volcanic mountain terrain reaching into the clouds of Highland Chiapas is the visible surface of the Zinacanteco world *Balamil*, which is conceived as a large quincunx in quadrilateral form (Vogt 1976). The center of the upper surface of this world is the "navel"—a low, rounded mound of earth located in the ceremonial center of Zinacantan. Nearby a shrine is maintained for offerings of candles, copal incense, and prayers to this "navel of the world" by Zinacantecos on pilgrimages to their ceremonial center. The whole world extends out from this "navel." Even Mexico City, the capital of the nation in which they live, is regarded by the Zinacantecos as a remote place off toward the edge of the world (see Gossen 1974).

The quincuncial world rests on the shoulders of the *Vashak-Men*, the local version of the "Four-Corner Gods" or "Sky-Bearers" who played an important role in the cosmology among the ancient Maya (Thompson 1934). When one of these gods tires and shifts the burden from one shoulder to another, an earthquake results and lasts until the burden is secure again. Since the population of the world is increasing, the burden frequently tires one or more of these gods. But the earthquakes kill enough people to lighten the burden and thus permit the gods to carry on their eternal duties.

K'atin-Bak ("place warmed by bones") is a deep hole, somewhere inside the earth, which is similar to the Christian Hell. It probably also contains elements of the prehistoric underworld (Vogt 1976).

Below the visible world, and separated from it by an open space, is the "Lower World" (Olon Balamil), also a quincunx. It is not as thick as the upper world and has more of the shape of a layer of an ancient Maya pyramid. The surface of this "Lower World" is inhabited by a race of dwarfs who, along with monkeys, were made in the mythological past when the gods unsuccessfully attempted to create real men.

In the Sky (Vinahel) above the earth is found the domain of the Sun, the Moon, and the Stars. The Sun, called "Our Father Heat," travels on a path that encircles the earth each day. Preceded by "the Sweeper of the Path," as Venus, the Morning Star, is called, the Sun appears each morning, pauses at high noon to survey the affairs of the Zinacantecos, and disappears each evening. As the Sun sets, it passes close to the ocean and makes the water boil. At night it continues on a path that passes between this world and the "Lower World," making it so hot for the dwarfs that they have to wear mud hats to protect themselves.

The path of the Sun provides the basic directions used by Zinacantecos for orienting themselves on the surface of the world. There is no abstract way of saying North, South, East, or West in Tzotzil. Instead our concept of East is approximated by words that translate as "place where the Sun rises," and West by "place where the Sun sets." What we regard as South and North are "the sides of the path of the Sun"; Zinacantecos differentiate the two by facing the "place where the Sun rises" and distinguishing between the right hand and the left hand. The "place where the Sun rises" is the primary direction for Zinacantecos, and most of their ceremonies have rituals that are oriented toward where "The Father Sun" makes his daily appearance.

The Moon, called "Our Holy Mother," travels on a similar path around the world, appearing here at night while the Sun is passing across the "Lower World." The Stars ("The Yellow Ones") are in a layer of the Sky above the clouds but below the paths of the Sun and Moon, providing light at night both above and below "like candles in the window of a house."

Under the influence of Spanish Catholicism, the Zinacantecos have come to associate the Sun with God the Father or Jesus Christ and the Moon with the Virgin Mary. But these associations have merely served to reinforce the ancient Mayan beliefs about the Sun and Moon as symbols of the contrasting maleness and femaleness in the universe.

The quincuncial model of the cosmos also influences the Zinacanteco view of—and ritual treatment of—their houses and fields. When a new house is completed and when a field is planted, the ceremonial circuits always proceed counter-clockwise around the four corners and end in the center, making offerings to the gods.

THE ANCESTORS

Almost all mountains (including smaller prominences we would call hills) located near Zinacanteco settlements are the homes of ancestral gods called "Fathers-Mothers". These ancestral gods are the most important Zinacanteco deities, judging from the frequency with which the people think about them, pray to them, and perform rituals for them. They are remote ancestors of the living Zinacantecos (no one can now trace direct genealogical connections with them), and they were ordered to take up residence inside the mountains by the Four-Corner Gods in the mythological past. They are pictured as looking and behaving as elderly Zinacantecos living eternally in their mountain homes, where they convene and deliberate, survey the affairs of their living descendants, and wait for the offerings of black chickens, candles, incense, and rum liquor which sustain them. Significantly enough, it is impossible to pray separately in Tzotzil to either a male ancestor or a female ancestor. The name *Totilme'il* may be literally translated as "Sir Father-Madam Mother," with the father image always linked to the mother image, indicating that the concept is a unitary one representing the primordial reproductive pair in the Zinacanteco universe.

In Zinacanteco view, these ancestors provide the ideal for human life—they know best how to grow corn, build houses, weave clothing, herd sheep, court and marry, cope with kinsmen, and perform ceremonies with all the necessary rituals. When living Zinacantecos perform ceremonies, they model their behavior upon what the ancestors are believed to be doing inside the mountains.

But the ancestors are not only repositories of the important social rules and cultural beliefs that compose the Zinacanteco way of life, they are also active and jealous guardians of the culture. Deviations are instantly noted, and guilty Zinacantecos are punished by means described below.

THE EARTH OWNER

Next to the ancestral gods, the most important deity is the "Earth Owner" (*Yahaval Balamil*). He has multiple manifestations: any large or small area on the earth may have an opening in the form of a cave, a limestone sink, or a waterhole (all called by one word—*ch'en*—in Tzotzil) that serves as a means of communication with him. He is pictured as a large, fat Ladino living under the ground with piles of money, herds of cows, mules, and horses, and flocks of chickens. He also owns all of the waterholes on which the Zinacantecos depend for household and livestock water; he controls the lightning and the clouds, which are believed to emerge from caves, rise up into the sky, and produce the needed rain for crops; and he controls all the products of the earth that Zinacantecos use—trees cut to build houses, mud used for the walls of the houses, limestone for lime, and so on. Hence, a Zinacanteco

Photo 1. Shaman (left) prays for a patient (right) to the Ancestral Gods who are believed to live inside mountains. The cross shrine is the means of communication with the Gods. Note incense burning (center) and bottle of liquor (front); also note similarity in shape of other sacred mountain (in background) to the pyramids in Ancient Maya sites. (Photo by Frank Cancian)

cannot use land, or any of its products, without compensating the Earth Owner with appropriate offerings in a ceremony.

The Earth Owner rides on deer, utilizing iguanas as blinders for his mounts and a snake for his whip. The shell of the land-snail is his powder flask for making sky rockets and for shooting his shotgun. Lightning bolts are the results of the firing of his rockets and his gun.

Communication with the Earth Owner is regarded with the deepest ambivalence. On the one hand, there are glorious myths about how men have acquired great wealth in money and livestock by going into caves to visit him. On the other hand, the Earth Owner needs many workers and there is always the danger that a man may be captured and forced to work in the earth until the iron sandals provided by the Earth Owner wear out.

THE SAINTS

In the centuries since the Spanish Conquest, the Zinacantecos have acquired over seventy sacred objects that they call "Saints" (*Santoeik*). Most of these are carved wooden or plaster images of Catholic saints, but many are pictures of saints and a few are large wooden crosses. The images range in size from less than 8 inches tall to full life-size. Forty-two of them are kept in three Catholic churches in Zinacantan Center; the others are found in houses of cargoholders (see Chapter 3) and in chapels in outlying hamlets. They are dressed in long, flowing robes derived from colonial styles, but almost all of them also have some item of typical Zinacanteco dress added to the Spanish costumes: the male saints have ribbons of the colors that are worn on men's hats; the female saints have necklaces, ribbons, and shawls like those worn by Zinacanteco women.

The most important saints have distinctive personalities and there are special myths explaining how they came to be in Zinacantan. *San Lorenzo* (Saint Lawrence) is now the main patron of Zinacantan. His image is in the place of honor over the main altar of the principal church. According to legend, San Lorenzo was found in the woods long ago by a Zinacanteco. His clothes were all torn and he was hungry. He told the Zinacanteco that he wanted to stay in Zinacantan and to please make this request to the *Presidente* at the *Cabildo* (the town hall). The request was granted; San Lorenzo was brought into the Center and a church built for him. When the church was finished, he entered his "home," where he now lives above the main altar. When he first arrived, San Lorenzo could talk. But the elders disapproved of "talking saints," so they threw hot water over him and silenced him forever.

San Sebastián (Saint Sebastian) occupies the place of honor over the center of the altar in the church named after him. He has a somewhat richer mythology attached to his past and also receives the most complex ritual during his fiesta in January. At least two mythological versions are related today by Zinacantecos concerning his origins. In one version San Sebastián was an officer in an army.

The king of the army wanted him to marry his daughter and San Sebastián refused. This enraged the king who ordered San Sebastián to be killed. San Sebastián fled, but the king's soldiers pursued him to Zinacantan where they killed him with their arrows. He carried two drums with him. At his death, one went into the cave at Nio'. At times it can still be heard playing there. The other [drum] is the one used during the fiesta for the saint. San Sebastián was buried where the church is now. Five years later some children taking care of sheep in the pasture found him sitting on Jaguar Rock. They went to tell the Presidente. The Presidente gathered the shamans, and with candles and incense, they went to talk to San Sebastián. When they arrived, he had gone, but he left a piece of paper saying that he wanted a church built so that he could live in Zinacantan. The shamans offered candles to the ancestors and to San Lorenzo to ask their advice. San Lorenzo then came and told the shamans not to worry, that their church would be built, and that the sun would be darkened for three days when the work was in progress. The temple was then built in three days, some Zinacantecos say by the Four Corner Gods. Others say that San Lorenzo was the supervisor of the work, while insects carried the rock, sand, and lime, and Santo Domingo mixed the cement. The Virgen del Rosario cut and carried the wood. The church was finished just as it stands today, and San Sebastián lives in it.

In the second version of the myth, San Sebastián was a captain of a group of soldiers in Oaxaca.

The king wanted him to marry his daughter, but San Sebastián refused. His refusal infuriated the king who ordered him to be shot. The soldiers took him outside the city, bound his hands behind him and shot him, but the bullets did not harm him. They next commissioned a group of Aztec or Lancandon Indians [for the informant, these are two names for the same people] to shoot him with arrows. San Sebastián fell mortally wounded, his body filled with arrows. San Lorenzo and Santo Domingo heard about this and went to Oaxaca to see what happened to San Sebastián. A Ladino merchant was traveling from Oaxaca to Comitan with his merchandise in an ox cart. He found San Sebastián by the side of the road. He put the saint on his ox cart thinking how fortunate he was to have the protection of a saint on his trip. On the second day of the journey, they arrived in Zinacantan, and camped for the night in the north pasture. San Sebastián decided to stay in Zinacantan. The next morning the merchant could not load San Sebastián back on the cart. He weighed too much, much more than he did before, and this was a sign that he wanted to remain. The merchant left, but animals came to guard San Sebastián: jaguars, birds, and two other types, one which is black. San Sebastián expressed his wish to remain. The people consulted San Lorenzo and Santo Domingo who knew what happened from their visit to Oaxaca. Thus the church in the north pasture was built. The same four types of animals still guard the church against anyone who should try to steal the saint from church.

Santo Domingo (Saint Dominic), whose image dwells just to the right of San Lorenzo over the main altar of the principal church, is a secondary patron. He was the main patron up to the end of the eighteenth century, but for reasons we do not yet know was replaced by San Lorenzo.

Santo Entierro, called *hmanvaneh* ("The Buyer") in Tzotzil, is a Christ-in-the-tomb image kept in an enclosed case to the right of the nave in the temple of San Lorenzo. According to the Zinacantecos, Santo Entierro used to live on earth. He was chased by demons who caught him and put him up on a cross in Zinacantan to kill him. When the demons went to eat, Santo Entierro came down from the cross. He took a blue rock and threw it high into the air, thus creating the blue sky. The demons returned from their meal and put him back on the cross where he died. In dying, he paid the price for our sins; this is why he is called "The Buyer." If he had not done this, we all would have died. Later he came back to life and went up into the sky to live.

Virgen del Rosario (Virgin of the Rosary) is called *ch'ulme'tik* ("Divine Mother") in Tzotzil. She is considered the patron of women in Zinacantan. She is sometimes identified as the moon, and as the mother of Santo Entierro.

Señor Esquipulas is a Christ-on-the-cross image kept in the Hermitage of Esquipulas where religious officials take their oaths of office. He is also associated with the salt trade, and ritual salt is delivered to the high ranking religious officials in his presence in the Hermitage.

This extraordinary collection of saints is clearly among the most sacred objects in Zinacantan, judging from the amount of ritual attention they receive, and from the resistance the Zinacantecos offer when outsiders try to see them or take photos of them. Hardly a fiesta occurs when at least one group of tourists is not forcibly evicted from a church for attempting to take photos, or when the Sacristanes do not shut and lock the church doors at the sight of approaching tourists.

The Zinacantecos think of them as gods with extraordinary power, each with an "inner soul" located in the image. Their "homes" are the Catholic churches. They must be bathed by water from the sacred waterholes and their clothes must be periodically washed and incensed—just as a patient in a curing ceremony is purified by being bathed and by having his clothes washed and incensed. Like the ancestral gods, they expect prayers and offerings of candles, incense, music, and flowers.

The Catholic Mass is considered by the Zinacantecos as an elaborate prayer for the saint whose fiesta is being celebrated. For the Zinacantecos, the saint "is a very human person who likes nice things." For his fiesta he very much wants the Mass with all the elaborate ornaments and vestments of the Catholic priest. If a Mass is not celebrated on his fiesta day, he is enraged and punishes whoever is responsible for this failure. Thus the Zinacantecos always go to San Cristobal to petition the priest for a Mass for every fiesta. If the priest comes, then the saint will have his "prayer." If the priest is otherwise occupied, and cannot come to say the Mass for fiesta, this does not upset the Zinacantecos. Their officials have accomplished their duty in asking for a Mass. The saint will still be enraged and send punishment, but he will punish the Catholic priest, not the Zinacantecos!

Whether or not the saints are replacements for particular indigenous idols that appeared in the aboriginal temples of the Zinacantecos at the time of the Conquest, we cannot yet say. In contemporary Zinacantan, ancestral gods and saints are integral parts of the pantheon and are treated ritually in much the same way.

The complex rituals performed for the saints by the officials will be described in a later chapter. But, in addition, family prayers to saints during fiestas are extremely important. Family groups, with the father carrying the candles and the flowers and the wife and children trailing behind, file continuously into the church during fiesta days. The image of the fiesta saint is usually placed in a prominent position. The family approaches as close as it can to the image, and the flowers are placed in a basket by the image or on the altar. Each member of the family then takes the hem of the saint's clothes into his hands, touches them to his forehead and kisses them. Then all kneel, light their candles, and place them on the floor in front of the image. The family remains kneeling and praying for fifteen to thirty minutes. The praying is emotionally intense, in high pitched tones, and there is often crying. Sometimes candles are purchased for all the saints in the church and the group then moves from saint to saint, offering candles and praying.

THE "SOULS"

Interaction between living Zinacantecos and their gods takes place via two types of "souls" that are possessed by each human being: a *ch'ulel* and a *chanul*. I use the term "soul" in quotes to indicate that the familiar European concepts of "souls" and "spirits" are inadequate for precise understanding of these ideas. In a very general way, of course, these Zinacanteco "souls" signify that the people are "animistic." But this statement tells us little about the subtle and complex meaning of "souls" or "vital forces" to the Zinacantecos.

The *ch'ulel* is an inner, personal "soul" located in the heart of each person; it is also found in the blood, which is known to be connected with the heart. It is placed in the body of an unborn embryo by the ancestral deities.

This Zinacanteco "inner soul" has some very special attributes. It is composed of thirteen parts, and a person who loses one or more parts must have a special curing ceremony to recover them. But the "inner soul," while temporarily divisible into parts in the various kinds of "soul-loss" that can occur, is believed to be eternal and indestructible. At the point of death the "inner soul" leaves the body. It is associated with the grave for a period of time corresponding to the length of the deceased person's life on earth, and then joins the "pool" of "inner souls" kept by the ancestors. It is later utilized for another person. But while the person is alive, the "inner soul" as a unit can leave the body during sleep and go visiting with "inner souls" of other Zinacantecos or the deities. It can also "drop out" of the body temporarily in periods of intense excitement, as in sexual intercourse. The "inner soul" tends especially to leave the body of a small child, as it is not yet used to this new receptacle. A mother with a small child in unfamiliar settings always sweeps the ground on which he has been sitting for a time with her shawl as she leaves, thereby making certain to gather up all the parts of the "inner soul" of her infant. Likewise, parents are expected to treat a small child with utmost care and affection, lest its "inner soul" become frightened and leave. One of the major purposes of the baptismal ceremony (see Chapter 6) is to "fix" the "inner soul" more firmly in the child's body.

However, even baptism does not prevent "soul-loss" from occurring through fright later in life. There are many immediate causes for "soul-loss"—falling down suddenly, seeing a "demon" on a dark night, and so on. The Zinacantecos still relate vividly how a large number of people experienced "soul-loss" when the first airplane swept low over Zinacantan about 40 years ago; the shamans were busy for weeks afterwards performing ceremonies to gather up pieces of "inner souls."

At a more profound level of causation, "soul-loss" is ordinarily believed to be due (a) to the ancestral gods, who punish bad behavior by causing a person to fall down, or, more dramatically, by sending a lightning bolt to knock out one or more parts of the "inner soul"; or (b) to an evil person who performs a witchcraft ritual in a cave to "sell" one or more parts of a victim's "inner soul" to the Earth Owner. The Earth Owner then proceeds to use the victim as a servant.

Without all thirteen parts of the "inner soul," a person cannot be healthy; he feels or possesses *chamel* ("sickness"). A shaman must be summoned to diagnose the sickness and to peform a ceremony to recover the missing parts and place them back into the body of the patient.

The phenomenon of the "inner soul" is by no means restricted to the domain of human beings. Virtually everything that is important and valuable to Zinacantecos also possesses an "inner soul": domesticated animals and plants such as maize, beans, squash; salt, which possesses a very strong "inner soul"; houses and household fires; the wooden crosses erected on sacred mountains, inside caves, and beside waterholes; the saints whose "homes" are inside the Catholic churches; musical instruments used in ceremonies; and all the various deities in the Zinacanteco pantheon. The ethnographer in Zinacantan soon learns that the most important interaction going on in the universe is not between persons, nor between persons and objects, as we think of these relationships, but rather between the "inner souls" inside these persons and material objects.

The second type of "soul" is the *chanul*, which is a kind of "animal spirit companion," or "spiritual alter ego," so to speak. Rising to over 9000 feet to the east of the Ceremonial Center is a majestic volcano called "Senior Large Mountain." A series of supernatural corrals containing 20,000 "animal spirit companions," one for each person in Zinacantan, are located inside the mountain. One corral contains jaguars, a second one coyotes, a third one ocelots, and a fourth one smaller animals like opossums. These "animal spirit companions" are watered, fed, and cared for by the ancestral gods, under the general supervision of the supernatural "Big Alcalde," the celestial counterpart of the highest ranking member of the religious hierarchy in Zinacantan. His house is located inside the mountain and his household cross is the shrine that Zinacantecos visit for ceremonies on top of the volcano.

The connection between the Zinacantecos and their "animal spirit companions" is made in their belief system by the idea that each person and his "animal spirit" share the same "inner soul." This means that when the ancestors install an "inner soul" in the embryo of a Zinacanteco, they simultaneously install the same "inner soul" in the embryo of an animal. Similarly, the moment that a Zinacanteco baby is born, a jaguar, coyote, ocelot, or other animal is born. Throughout life, whatever happens of note to the Zinacanteco happens to his "animal spirit companion" and vice versa. If, for example, an "animal spirit companion" is let out of the corral and left to wander alone in the forest, it may be injured or shot, and then his Zinacanteco counterpart feels the same injury. It follows that if the "animal spirit companion" is let out of the corral and is thereby not being cared for properly by the ancestors, a Zinacanteco is in mortal danger. A shaman must be summoned and must proceed with dispatch to perform the proper ceremony, asking the pardon of the ancestral deities and persuading them to round up the lost "animal spirit companion" of the patient and place it safely back in its supernatural corral.

It is ordinarily sometime during childhood when Zinacantecos discover what kind of "animal spirit companion" they have, and they usually receive this knowledge in a dream when their "inner soul" is off visiting and "sees" their "animal spirit" when it visits the ancestral gods inside "Senior Large Mountain."

There is a clear relationship between the beliefs in these two "soul" concepts and social control in the Zinacanteco code of life. For anything that stirs up the wrath of the ancestors against a particular Zinacanteco can lead quickly and directly to punishment (a) by causing the person to suffer "soul-loss," or (b) in more serious cases, by having his "animal spirit companion" turned outside its corral to wander alone and uncared for in the woods. The types of deviant behavior that can lead to these "soul" troubles include, significantly enough, the breaking of important moral rules or the flouting of the central values of Zinacantan. For example, an individual who fights with or mistreats his kinsmen; a man who fails to accept the community service in the religious hierarchy; a man who fails to care for his maize field properly or a woman who mishandles the maize after it is brought to her house; a person who fails to wash regularly and change into clean clothes; or a man who fails to make contributions when the officials arrive to collect "taxes" for fiestas—are all prime candidates for sickness caused by "soul" troubles.

There is also a fundamental way in which the concept of the "animal spirit companion" relates Zinacantecos in an intimate way to the world of nature (see Levi-Strauss 1966). Zinacantecos make an important distinction between the areas used and controlled by human beings, such as houses, patios, waterholes, and fields, and the wild, wooded slopes of the Chiapas mountains, which are not under human control. All of the "animal spirit companions" are "animals of the forest." The concept of the "animal spirit companions" forges a connection between the dichotomous parts of their universe. It creates an intimate relationship between the lives of humans and the lives of wild animals inhabiting the wooded slopes of the mountains. And in these same high mountains dwell the ancestral gods who survey the affairs of the Zinacanteco descendants and exercise maximal control over their behavior by either care or neglect of the 20,000 "animal spirit companions" upon whom living Zinacantecos absolutely depend for continuing survival.

THE CROSSES

Casual visitors to Zinacantan always come away with the impression that they must have visited one of the most solidly Catholic communities in the world. There are literally hundreds of apparently Christian wooden crosses in Zinacantan—not only on churchtops and in churchyards, but in the patios outside houses, beside all waterholes, at the foot of and on top mountains, and in caves.

When Zinacantecos describe these crosses in Tzotzil, they use the word *krus*, an obvious loan-word from the Spanish term for cross. But while these may look like contemporary replicas of the classic Christian cross on which Christ was crucified in far off Jerusalem, they have no such meaning to the Zinacantecos.

When I initiated my fieldwork in Zinacantan in 1956, I was shown the hill above the Ceremonial Center containing a large and elaborate cross shrine and was told it was *Kalvaryo*. Since in that first season Zinacantan appeared to me to be a peasant community that had been converted to Catholicism in the 1500's, I was not surprised to find a "Calvary" near the churches in the Ceremonial Center. Later I discovered that black chickens were left as a sacrifice by curing parties at this *Kalvaryo*. I gradually learned that the ancestral gods are believed to have meetings at the *Kalvaryo* just as officials meet at the Cabildo in the Center. By the second and third seasons, it had become more and more apparent that Zinacantecos were not Catholic peasants with a few Maya remnants left in the culture, but rather that they were Maya tribesmen with a Spanish Catholic veneer—a veneer that appears to be increasingly thin the longer we do fieldwork with the culture. The final shock came when I discovered in early 1960 that there is not one, but hundreds of *Kalvaryos* in Zinacantan, located throughout the *municipio* in all hamlets. Thus the Zinacanteco view of *Kalvaryo* gradually became clear: it is a special type of cross shrine where particular groups of ancestral gods are believed to meet, deliberate about the affairs of their living descendants, and wait for offerings of black chickens, white candles, and rum. It also became clear that they symbolize units of social structure and are related to the ancestral deities responsible for these units. The original *Kalvaryo* I was shown proved to represent the meeting place of the tribal (or all-municipio) ancestral gods who live in mountains around the Ceremonial Center. The other *Kalvaryos* represented in each case a lineage or a waterhole group—the units that I shall describe in Chapter 4. What appeared at first to be contemporary replicas of the ancient Christian Calvary proved to be ancestral shrines representing units of social structure at various levels, where Zinacantecos go to pray and leave offerings to their ancestral gods who are meeting there and waiting eagerly for the prayers and offerings. In a word, the *Kalvaryos* mirror the social system—a social system with deep roots in the Mayan past.

Each of the mountain dwelling places of the ancestral gods is now marked by the erection of crosses. Around the Center there are cross altars both at the foot and on top of each of the tribal sacred mountains. The Zinacanteco view of these crosses is that they are "doorways" to the ancestral gods. For example, when a curing procession arrives at a sacred mountain, the members, led by the shaman, decorate the crosses with pine boughs and flowers, burn incense, light candles, and offer prayers to the crosses at the foot of the mountain. By so doing, they "pass through" the outer doorway of the house and from there proceed up the trail to the top of the mountain, where another set of crosses designates the patio cross for the house of the ancestral god who is sitting inside to receive his visitors and their offerings. Here the ritual is repeated and then the curing party proceeds to the next mountain on their circuit.

Similarly, the crosses erected beside waterholes and in caves are defined as channels of communication with the Earth Owner, and it is by way of these cross shrines that he receives his offerings of candles and liquor. The cross erected in the patio outside Zinacanteco houses is an entry way into the "essence," that is, the "inner soul" of the house. In any kind of ceremony, entrance into or departure from the house is invariably accomplished by specific prayers at this cross.

For any kind of ritual activity a *Krus* must be triple to be effective. Many cross shrines contain in fact only one wooden cross (as in the case of the house cross); some contain only two wooden crosses (as in the case of many shrines at foot or on top of the sacred mountains). But these are ritually converted into a triple cross by the addition of pinetree tops at the sides of the one, or two, wooden crosses. Further, I have noted that if no wooden crosses exist at a place where ritual must be performed (for example, a spot where a part of an "inner soul" has been lost), the three-cross combination can be created ritually by simply placing three pinetree tops in the ground. This has led me to the conclusion that the wooden cross is for the Zinacantecos simply a handy structure on which to place the crucial pinetree tops and flowers that are necessary symbols.

For any kind of ritual activity in Zinacantan that involves communication with the gods, a set of symbols are utilized to provide a sacred context in which the communication can take place. These symbolic elements clearly define the situation and set the stage for the performance of "ritual" as opposed to "technical" activity (see Turner 1967). Each day Zinacantecos perform many "technical" activities, such as hoeing maize, weaving, herding sheep, and so forth, which may involve taboos of various types, but which are clearly differentiated from "ritual" activities, in which offerings are to be made to supernaturals. Three of the symbolic elements—flowers, copal incense, and rum—are invariable aspects of the "ritual" situation. A fourth, the playing of music, is added to particular ritual events.

Although we often translate nichim as "flower," following the lead of Spanish-speaking Zinacantecos who describe these plants as *flores*, it is clear that the Tzotzil category *nichim* includes much more than we conventionally think of as "flowers"—for example, the young, freshly grown tops of pine trees as well as pine needles, and a variety of other plants.

The cross shrine is prepared by tying three pinetree tops to the three crosses, or by making three crosses with the addition of the pinetree tops (as described above). The red geranium blossoms (and other plants, which vary with the type of ceremony) are then tied in bundles to the pine tops at the level of the cross arms of the crosses, and a fresh, green carpet of pine needles is laid down in front of the shrine.

Not only must the "doorway" be readied with the flowers, but incense must also be burning in a censer for effective communication with the supernaturals to take place. The censer is called a "place of burning embers" and the incense that is burned is of two types: balls of resin and chips of wood. Both types are burned together in the censer, and the incense must be burning at the cross before the ritual party arrives and begins the prayers. For example, for a house cross to be ready for a curing ceremony, it must have the incense burning in a censer in front of it when the shaman arrives at the house to begin the ceremony. Similarly, the burning censer is carried in the procession to the sacred mountains and placed in front of the cross shrines before the shaman begins to light candles and pray.

With the flowers in place and the incense burning, the participants must also be readied for communication with the supernaturals, and the most important way to prepare is to drink liquor. For just as any important communication or transaction among people (borrowing money, asking a man to serve as godfather for a child, asking for a wife, etc.) is accompanied by the drinking of rum, so must transactions between humans and their supernaturals be accompanied by the proper consumption of this liquor. This rum, called *posh* (meaning literally "medicine"), is an inexpensive rum distilled from brown sugar.

A highly patterned sequence of behavior is involved in a drinking ritual, a sequence that is followed, with minor variations, whether the occasion is a small curing ceremony within the domestic group or a large change-of-office ceremony performed by the cargoholders in the Ceremonial Center. A young man designated as "drink pourer" is given the bottle of liquor and a shot glass. He pours a glassful and hands it to the senior male present. The senior male accepts the glass, holds it in his left hand, and engages in toasting and in bowing-and-releasing behavior with all the others present. The toast consists of his raising the shot glass and saying kich'ban ("I drink," followed by a kin term or name) to each person—in rank order—and receiving from each person the response of "icho" ("Drink"). The toasting is accompanied by

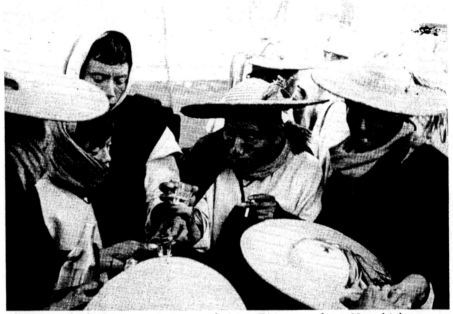

Photo 2. A drinking ceremony in progress during a Zinacanteco fiesta. Note drink-pourer at left. (Photo by Frank Cancian)

bowing and releasing—that is, each person bows his head toward the senior man and is released by the senior man touching the back of his right hand to his forehand. The senior man then drinks the shot in one gulp, grimaces to show how strong the liquor is, spits a few drops on the floor, and returns the glass to the "drink pourer" who proceeds to serve the next man in rank order. The next man repeats the toast and the bowing and releasing—that is, he bows to the more senior man, but all others bow to him and are released. The sequence is repeated in the rank order, from the eldest to the youngest male, then continuing with the most senior female present until all have been served. Then the "pourer" takes a shot last and goes through the toasting and bowing and releasing behavior. The rounds normally proceed in threes. If, for example, a bottle of liquor is presented by a visitor asking for a loan of money, it should be consumed in three rounds. If, on the other hand, the occasion is a ritual meal for a curing ceremony, there are normally three rounds during the course of the meal. It is up to the "pourer" to make careful calculations so that the entire bottle will be consumed in three rounds. While rank order is strictly observed in the serving of liquor, each person present should receive equal amounts.

This strict insistence upon rank order in the sequence of serving the liquor, but upon equal amounts being received by each participant is symbolically significant. The symbolic message being communicated is that while Zinacanteco society has a rank order based mainly upon age, but also upon prestige accorded to shamans and/or men who have passed cargos, *every* person in the society is expected to receive *equal* amounts of drink and food regardless of rank.

An interesting custom for handling excess liquor is brought into play when a person becomes intoxicated or no longer wishes to drink. Men ordinarily carry an empty bottle, along with a small metal funnel attached by buckskin to the bags they carry over their shoulders. They go through all the toasting and bowing and releasing behavior, touch the glass to their lips, but instead of drinking the liquor, use the funnel to pour the liquor into their empty bottles. Women do not carry this equipment, but instead pour the liquor into a bowl near the *metates* where they are working by the fire in the house.

For all of the important public ceremonies music is an essential ingredient. During a major fiesta in the Ceremonial Center, four types of music are often being played simultaneously—an experience that jars the nerves of visiting ethnographers, but which, from a Zinacanteco point of view, adds importance and gaiety to the fiesta. Two of these represent aspects of the more secular parts of the fiesta: (1) the music from loud-speakers blaring out Mexican songs played on record players in the *cantinas*, and (2) the sounds of a hired brass band that plays in the kiosk while the men dance in the evenings, and also accompanies groups of "volunteers" who march from their homes to the church to present special offerings of candles to the saints. The Ladino musicians walk from their towns, but young Zinacantecos are appointed to carry their instruments. It is always a startling experience to see a Zinacanteco in full fiesta regalia, with new ribbons flowing from his hat, crossing the Pan American Highway carrying a tuba!

The other two sources of music are, however, much more important ritually: (1) the flute and drum group, always consisting of one flautist and two drummers, and used to accompany processions of various types, and (2) the violin, harp, and guitar combination (with the instruments ranked in the order listed) that plays for certain ceremonial occasions. The instruments used are made by Chamulas. They are based on Spanish colonial models, but are crude reflections of the originals. For example, the violin has three pegs but only two strings. The music played appears to be derived from early Spanish colonial tunes the Zinacantecos learned after the Conquest.

With flowers on the crosses, incense burning vigorously in a censer, liquor being consumed by the participants, and music being played by musicians, the stage is set for efficient communication with the supernaturals through prayers and offerings, typically candles, which are regarded as tortillas and meat for the gods, and black chickens, whose "inner souls" are eagerly consumed by the gods. As the candles burn down, it is believed that the "souls" of the candles are providing the necessary sustenance, along with the "souls" of the black chickens, for the supernaturals, who will be so pleased with these offerings that they will reciprocate by restoring the "inner soul" of the patient, by sending rain for a thirsty maize crop, or by eliminating any number of evils and setting things right for the Zinacantecos.

3/The Ceremonial Center and The Hamlets

Zinacantan is a classic example of an ancient type of Maya settlement pattern: a ceremonial center with a sustaining area of outlying hamlets in which most of the people live (see Map 2). In Classic Maya times the major ceremonial centers contained the pyramids, the stelae, the palaces, the causeways, the plazas, and other ritual structures. In the outlying hamlets there were also usually smaller pyramids that served as minor ceremonial centers for the people in the hamlets. The hamlets in turn were subdivided into "cluster groups," "clusters," and "patio groups" that were probably the residential aggregations of successively smaller units in a kin-based system of patriclans, patrilineages, and patrilocal extended families (Vogt 1983).

Contemporary Zinacantan has a ceremonial center, called *Hteklum* ("My Real Land") in Tzotzil, and twenty-six outlying *parajes*, as the hamlets are called in Chiapas. Approximately 2500 people live in the Ceremonial Center; the other 17,500 live in the hamlets. The Mexican *municipio* structure has been imposed upon this ancient pattern so that the Ceremonial Center is now the *cabecera* ("headquarters") where political as well as religious officials serve their tours of duty; temples have been replaced by Catholic churches; and there is a *cabildo* ("town hall"). Social life in the hamlets, organized in domestic groups, localized lineages, and waterhole groups (described in the next chapter), has changed less. Many of the hamlets now have Catholic chapels, but otherwise the basic settlement pattern seems to have changed little since the time of the Conquest.

THE CEREMONIAL CENTER

The Ceremonial Center is located in a well-watered valley at 7000 feet and surrounded by a series of impressive mountains. The streets are laid out in a grid pattern—a feature not found in the hamlets. There are three Catholic churches: San Lorenzo (which houses the patron saint and is the largest and most important), San Sebastián (connected by a path, resembling an ancient causeway, with San Lorenzo), and the Hermitage of Señor Esquipulas (located on one side of the churchyard in front of San Lorenzo). The town hall, with the jail behind it, is located across the street from the churchyard of San

Photo 3. The Church of San Lorenzo in Zinacantan Center during a major fiesta.
(Photo by Frank Cancian)

Lorenzo. Nearby is a Mexican government school and clinic, and about twenty small stores, all but one now owned by Zinacantecos.

At the upper end of the valley, the last large Ladino ranch has been taken over by Zinacantecos and Chamulas as part of the Mexican agrarian reform program. The result is a town that is much more Indian in population and character than it was 70 years ago when a substantial Ladino population both lived in and had more control over Zinacantan Center.

Of utmost importance to the Zinacantecos are the sacred places in and around the Ceremonial Center, especially the mountains, waterholes, and cross shrines. It is these sacred places that symbolically represent tribal as opposed to hamlet gods and that require the presence of Zinacantecos in their Ceremonial Center even when they are not serving in official positions or conducting business at the town hall.

The five most important sacred mountains are *Bankilal Muk'ta Vits* ("Senior Large Mountain"), where the "animal spirit companions" are kept in their supernatural corrals by the ancestral gods, and four mountains that are regularly visited by curing parties who come to the Ceremonial Center to pray to the ancestors: *Kishotoval Vits* ("San Cristobal Mountain"), *Mushul Vits* ("Snub-Nosed Mountain"), *Sisil Vits* ("Santa Cecilia Mountain"), and *Kalvaryo* ("Calvary"). As I indicated in the last chapter, this latter mountain is conceived as the meeting place of the tribal ancestral gods. In addition, there are seven sacred waterholes in which the ancestral gods are believed to take their baths and from which water must be drawn for curing ceremonies. Finally, there are cross shrines at street corners around the edges of the core of the Ceremonial Center that figure importantly in the ceremonies performed by the cargoholders (see below).

THE CARGO SYSTEM

The key feature of the social structure of the Ceremonial Center is a "religious hierarchy," organized basically around the Catholic churches and saints (see Cancian 1965). When a Zinacanteco speaks of *'abtel ta Hteklum*, he is referring to the important "work" or "service" provided by men who hold positions in this hierarchy. *'Abtel* is conceived of as bearing a burden, much as a Zinacanteco carries a heavy load of maize on his back. But in the context of carrying burdens in the Ceremonial Center, the concept is probably related to the ancient Maya idea of the "Year Bearer," especially since the positions are held for one year. Like the ancient Maya gods who carried the "year" with a tumpline and passed it along to their successors, a contemporary Zinacanteco carries the burden of the office for a year and then passes it along to his successor. In Spanish these positions came to be called cargos. While the positions are conceived as burdens, they also provide enormous prestige for the cargoholders and hence are much sought by Zinacanteco men.

This religious hierarchy, or cargo system, in Zinacantan consists of sixty-one positions in four levels in a ceremonial ladder. To pass through this

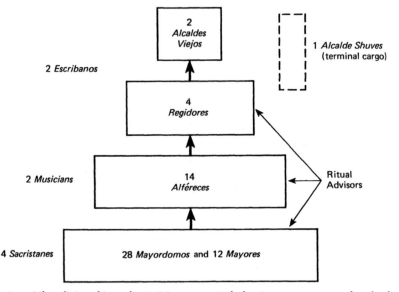

Figure 3-1. The religious hierarchy in Zinacantan includes sixty-one cargos on four levels and four types of important auxiliary personnel. (adapted from Cancian 1965:29)

ceremonial ladder a man must serve a year at each level, and during the time he holds a cargo, he is expected to move from his hamlet into the Ceremonial Center and engage in a complex annual round of ceremonies. The ceremonies are quite expensive, some cargos costing the incumbents as much as can be earned in four years of wages for food, liquor, and ritual paraphernalia such as candles, incense, and fireworks. To provide some idea of what this means, my colleague Frank Cancian has calculated that it is equivalent to my having to take leave-of-absence from Harvard without pay for a year and to spend some $75,000 U.S. during the year in ceremonial activity!

While he fills the role, a cargoholder wears special costumes and enjoys special prestige. At the end of the year, he turns the post over to the next incumbent, and moves back to his hamlet to become a full time maize farmer again. Some years must elapse before he can work himself out of debt and accumulate enough wealth to ask for a cargo position on the next higher level. When he completes all four cargos, he finally becomes an honored *pasado*.

The first level contains several alternatives; for the sake of simplicity I have divided these into *Mayores* and *Mayordomos*. The twelve Mayores, who are ranked from one to twelve, serve as policemen and errand boys for the civil officials at the Cabildo, but they also have important ceremonial functions that will be described later. The twenty-eight Mayordomos care for particular saints in the Catholic churches in the Center, or in one of the chapels in the outlying hamlets. Their cargos are named after the principal saint they serve— the Mayordomos of San Sebastián, the Mayordomos of Santo Domingo, and so on. The twelve Mayordomos who serve the saints in the churches of San

Photo 4. Top-ranking cargoholders in front of Cabildo in Zinacantan Center. From the left, the Big and Little Alcaldes, the two Scribes and the four Regidores. (Photo by Frank Cancian)

Lorenzo and San Sebastián in the Center are organized into two ranked orders: Senior and Junior. Thus, there are the Senior and Junior Mayordomo of San Sebastián on up to the Senior and Junior Mayordomo of Sacramento who serve the patron, San Lorenzo. The fourteen *Alféreces* are also named for saints and organized into two ranked orders: Senior and Junior. Although they once may have had crucial caretaking duties for the saints, they now spend most of their year in office feeding one another at ritual meals and dancing for the saints. The four *Regidores* are also ranked, one to four. With the two *Alcaldes Viejos*, who are also ranked into the "Big" and "Little" Alcalde, the Regidores form a group at the top of the hierarchy known collectively as the *Moletik*, the "Elders." It is the duty of the "Elders" to manage the cargo system. In addition, the Regidores have the duty of collecting money to pay the Catholic priests for saying Masses.

It is interesting that for an old man who has not managed to serve at each level, there is one position, that of *Alcalde Shuves*, to which he can be appointed as a terminal cargo when it is evident he is not going to be able to aspire to a top Alcalde Viejo post.

Another crucial feature of the hierarchy is the functioning of the *Totilme'iletik*. These Ritual Advisors bear the same name as the ancestral deities. Just as the supernatural *Totilme'iletik* give advice and direct ceremonies inside

Photo 5. The four Regidores praying in front of the Church of San Lorenzo in Zinacantan Center. (Photo by Frank Cancian)

their mountain homes, so the living *Totilme'iletik* in Zinacantan Center give cargoholders technical ritual advice on how to carry out their duties. Each cargoholder in the first three levels recruits a Ritual Advisor to help him with the complicated ritual during his year in office. The man selected for the role must have passed at least two cargos, and is chosen for his ability to talk well in ritual situations and to direct ritual.

While each of the cargo positions is of one-year duration, the auxiliary personnel who perform key duties in the Ceremonial Center and assist the cargo-holders serve for longer periods of time. These include the four *Sacristanes* ("Sacristans"), whose daily duties include opening and closing the churches and ringing the bells at 6 A.M., Noon, and 6 P.M. and whose more extensive duties are to assist the Mayordomos with ritual for the saints; the two *Musicos* ("Musicians"), a violinist and a harpist, who play for the Alféreces and provide ritual advice for these second level cargoholders; and the two *Escribanos* ("Scribes"), who are attached to the "Elders" at the top two levels of the hierarchy and whose duty it is to keep records of taxes for fiestas and of appointments to cargo posts.

With the Ritual Advisors serving as "masters of ceremonies" and the auxiliary personnel serving as constantly available ritual consultants, the Zinacantecos are able to maintain and transmit a very complex set of ceremonies (see Chapter 7) with a system of annually rotating positions in their religious hierarchy.

THE CABILDO

While the cargoholders are managing the ceremonial life of Zinacantan Center, the civil officials are performing their duties in the Cabildo across the street. These officials are also ranked: from the *Presidente* through the *Síndico*, the four *Alcaldes Jueces*, and the nine civil *Regidores*, who traditionally sat in rank order on a long bench on the front porch of the Cabildo, to the left of the door. To the right of the door the Mayores, serving as the policemen and errand boys, sat on another long bench. Inside, seated behind a desk with an imposing-looking typewriter, sat the *Secretario*, the only Ladino to occupy a position in the civil government of Zinacantan. Behind his desk is an ancient telephone which connects him with the officials in San Cristobal, but it is used only in an emergency. And, in fact, the everyday governmental affairs are managed by the Indian officials, while the Ladino Secretary merely keeps the town records.

Recently, the town hall has been renovated. The Indian officials now sit inside where it is drier and warmer. The Presidente, the Jueces, and the Regidores sit in rank order from East to West behind a large desk in an office on the eastern side of the Cabildo. The Secretary sits behind a desk in an office on the western side, indicating from the Zinacanteco point of view that he is clearly of lesser rank than the Indian officials in their office on the East. The Mayores are now seated on benches and awaiting their calls to duty in a hallway located between the two offices.

These civil officials serve three-year terms, and in Mexican Government theory they are "elected" to office. In fact, they are selected for office by the leading *Cacique* ("political boss") of Zinacantan. The previous most important Cacique was an energetic and intelligent Zinacanteco who had controlled the *ejido* committee for almost thirty years. His power was based mainly upon this control of the ejido land that the Zinacantecos acquired with the agrarian reform program. The current Caciques of Zinacantan have different power bases; one is the Pepsi-Cola distributor for the municipio; others own many trucks and Volkswagen microbuses which provide transportation for people and goods to and from the markets in San Cristobal and Tuxtla Gutierrez and to and from the rented fields in the Grijalva Valley where the Zinacantecos grow most of their maize.

While the civil officials have a variety of functions, including greeting visiting Ladino officials, collecting money for and supervising public works (such as repairing roads and bridges), carrying out a few ritual functions, and appointing committees for fiestas, their major duties are concerned with disputes among Zinacantecos. Day after day, the Presidente, the Síndico, and at least one of the Jueces and one of the Regidores (who rotate the duty) sit behind their desk in the Cabildo and wait for law cases. If the Presidente is absent, the Síndico takes the Presidente's silver-headed baton (containing a strong "inner soul" placed there by the ancestral gods), moves over to the number one position behind the desk, and hears the cases.

While some Zinacantecos seek the Presidente out at his house at night so that they can have an uninterrupted hearing of their cases, the more common procedure is for the plaintiff to approach the Presidente at the Cabildo. The plaintiff bows to the Presidente and other officials in rank order, presents a bottle of rum, and describes his complaint. The Presidente and other officials listen, and, if persuaded, summon two of the Mayores to go after the accused and bring him into the Cabildo. The defendant appears, also with a bottle of rum, bows to the officials, and presents his defense. Usually, both parties, accompanied by relatives known to be "good talkers" who serve as "lawyers," all talk at once and one wonders how in the ensuing pandemonium a judgment is ever reached. Witnesses may be called on both sides to provide additional testimony.

The case may have one of three outcomes: (1) it may be settled in this Zinacanteco court, with the officials helping to the extent of expressing their approval of an argument or hooting with laughter at a defendant who is telling an obvious lie (in this case the culprit will be required to return the stolen property and be fined, or jailed, or both); (2) the case may prove too serious for the Zinacanteco court to handle (for example, a case of murder) and is passed along to the Ladino officials in San Cristobal; or (3) it may be impossible to reach a clear-cut decision, even after all the testimony is heard, and then the Presidente's efforts are devoted to calming down the two parties so they will not bear grudges against each other and will be able to live harmoniously in the same hamlet.

THE HAMLETS

Zinacantan's hamlets are recognized officially in two ways. First, they are units for the Mexican census taken every decade. Second, each hamlet has at least one, and normally two, *Principales* whose duty it is to represent the Cabildo in their hamlets. One or both normally report to the Presidente each Sunday in the Ceremonial Center; they carry official messages to their hamlets; they collect taxes to help pay for major fiestas; and they also have some ritual duties, especially at the Year Renewal Ceremonies (see Chapter 7).

Each hamlet is named, its borders are clearly known to its inhabitants, and each is said by the Zinacantecos to have special characteristics. They range in size from 120 people to 3160 (1989 estimate). I shall briefly describe six of the more important hamlets to provide a picture of their principal features.

NABENCHAUK, the largest hamlet, is concentrated in a beautiful mountain valley. Around the perimeter of the valley are a number of precipitous limestone hills, and the valley bottom contains a relatively large number of springs and waterholes. The valley drains into a lake at the southwest corner, and the lake in turn drains out through a fissure in the limestone, or so-called *sumidero*. This lake is believed to be Nabenchauk, or "the lake of the lightning," and provides the name for the hamlet. The Pan American Highway skirts the northern edge of the valley as it passes from Tuxtla Gutierrez to San Cristobal, giving Nabenchauk a major means of transportation for people and maize. It also makes possible the sale of flowers, which are either sold locally by small boys who hold up bunches and attempt to flag down passing cars to sell their products, or transported to the markets in San Cristobal, or, more especially, to Tuxtla Gutierrez.

The hamlet contains a school, a Catholic chapel dedicated to the Virgen de Guadalupe, a number of stores, and a Cabildo, where various civil officials cope with local problems of law and order. Nabenchauk has been an *agencia* for some years and hence has its own local civil officials. There has been constant pressure in recent years to become independent of Zinacantan Center, and this political pressure has been important in the formation of two major factions that are constantly contending with each other for power and influence within the hamlet.

PASTE', located in high terrain south of the Pan American Highway, is the most dispersed hamlet. Elevations range from 7000 to 8000 feet, with an average of 7500. The name of the hamlet derives from its largest waterhole, *vo'ta paste'*, which is located on the southern border where the land begins to fall off in a descent of over 6000 feet into the lowlands of the Grijalva River. Two explanations of the origin of the name (*pas te'* means "chunk of wood") are possible: some people say the earlier settlers around the waterhole were noted for working with wood products; others attribute the name to the presence of a sacred tree beside the waterhole placed there by the ancestral god who found the waterhole in the mythological past.

Paste' is noted for having a relatively large number of special ceremonial items and ritual specialists, whose services or products are needed in cargo ceremonies in Zinacantan Center, and for the duty it has to supply lime for municipal public works. The hamlet has a school and a Catholic chapel. It has a population of 2580.

VO'CH'OH VO' ("Five Waterholes") is a hamlet of 2540 people, located in the upper or eastern end of the valley of Zinacantan and extending over the hills that separate it from the hamlet of Na Chih to the South. The portion located in the valley of Zinacantan has a relatively compact settlement pattern (like Nabenchauk), but the house groups are more dispersed in the higher elevations toward Na Chih. The hamlet is in the process of fissioning into two hamlets which reflect these differences.

NA CHIH ("House of the Sheep"), with a population of 2140, is the fourth largest hamlet of Zinacantan. It is located in a mountain valley between Vo'ch'oh Vo' on the north and Paste' on the south. Unlike the valley of Nabenchauk, the valley is open to the west and drains into a precipitous *barranca* that carries the water down into the lowlands through the neighboring municipio of Ixtapa. The dispersal of houses is intermediate, between the more compact pattern found in Nabenchauk or 'Apas and the more scattered pattern found in Paste'. The hamlet contains a large federal school and a number of Indian-owned stores, as well as a Catholic chapel, and is, like Vo'ch'oh Vo', in the process of fissioning into two hamlets.

Since the Pan American Highway bisects the hamlet, it is more profoundly affected by this transportation artery than any other Zinacanteco hamlet. The highway has its advantages for the people of Na Chih, but it also has its hazards. Since the road passing through Na Chih is a straight run for over a mile, cars roar through the hamlet at high speeds, and not infrequently strike sheep, mules, horses, and children on the highway. A number of years ago, after two children were killed, the people of Na Chih moved to "encapsulate" this section of the Pan American Highway into their ritual system in order to cancel out the "evil." Cross shrines were erected beside the highway where it enters and leaves the hamlet, and a special ceremonial circuit is now performed each year, with the shamans saying prayers and making offerings to the ancestral gods to attempt to offset the hazards of this modern invasion of their hamlet by the twentieth-century transportation system.

'APAS (meaning obscure) with a population of 1400, is substantially smaller than the four hamlets described above, and is one of the most compactly settled hamlets. It is located about an hour by trail or half-hour by road southwest of Nabenchauk and is at least 500 feet lower in elevation. Its houses are located on a relatively flat bench wedged in between a rim of limestone mountains to the south and a series of precipitous barrancas on the north. The site contains twelve waterholes, providing ample water for the population and livestock. The hamlet now contains a few small stores and there is a school house and a Catholic chapel devoted to Señor Esquipulas.

'ATS'AM ("salt"), called *Salinas* in Spanish, is one of the most interesting and distinctive hamlets. It is located at the bottom of a very precipitous barranca west of Zinacantan Center and near the route of the ancient wagon road that connected Ixtapa with the Center and San Cristobal. The hamlet is relatively small (population 740), and the houses are compactly located in a small space wedged between the walls of the barranca.

The most distinctive feature of 'Ats'am is the presence of a sacred salt well located next to the Catholic chapel. Special rituals are performed in connection with this salt which is processed for household use for residents of the hamlet and is transported in small quantities to Zinacantan Center as gifts for the high-ranking cargoholders.

Photo 6. The hamlet of 'Apas nestles on a mountain bench between a deep canyon (on the left) and a precipitous ridge (on the right). (Photo by the Compañía Mexicana Aerofoto)

THE SHAMANS

While the cargoholders are performing the annual round of ceremonies in the Center, other ceremonial practitioners are carrying out rituals in the hamlets—the *h'iloletik* or "shamans." The term *h'ilol* means literally "seer." Zinacantecos believe that in ancient mythological times all people could "see" into the mountains and observe the ancestral gods directly, but that now only the shamans can accomplish this miracle. There are at least 250 shamans in Zinacantan. Most are men, but some are women, and some are as young as fifteen years of age. To become a shaman a person dreams three times that his "inner soul" has been called before the ancestral gods in the "Senior Large Mountain." In the first dream, which usually occurs when a person is ten or twelve, the "inner soul" of a supernatural *Mayor* appears and directs the "inner soul" of the novice to come with him to the house of the Alcalde inside the mountain. Upon arrival, the novice is conducted inside the house where the supernatural Big Alcalde is seated at the east end of a long table flanked by all of the shamans in Zinacantan in order of their rank. The novice kneels at the west end of the table after bowing to all of those present. The Alcalde asks him if he is prepared to become a shaman. He has to say "yes"; otherwise he will die. Then the novice receives all the types of candles and flowers required for a curing ceremony and is given instructions on how to say the proper prayers and perform the ritual. He is also given a ceremonial robe to don, and he kneels again while the Alcalde makes the sign of the cross on his forehead to swear him in. A patient is then brought in, and the novice must diagnose the illness and perform the proper ceremony while the Big Alcalde and all the shamans observe his performance.

In the second and third dreams, which usually occur about a year apart, the process is completed, but the patients which the novice must cure are different. For example, if the patient in his first dream was an old man, it may be a woman in his second dream, a child in his third dream. The novice now possesses the necessary knowledge, and he makes his public debut as a shaman sometime afterwards, typically when he himself falls ill and knows by this signal that he must respond to the "call." To make his public debut he goes to the highest ranking shaman in the hamlet in which he lives and tells him his dreams and asks permission to reveal himself as a shaman. The older shaman prays to all the ancestral gods in the sacred mountains and gives permission. The novice then goes to the lowlands to cut a bamboo staff, which he will henceforth always carry in his left hand as a symbol of his office. Returning to his home, he tells his relatives about his new ritual power, and they begin to call upon him to perform ceremonies. He thus becomes a full-fledged shaman.

Perhaps the most surprising feature about the shamans in Zinacantan is that they are all ranked in order from 1 to 250. Rank order depends not upon age or power, but upon time in service—that is, the number of years that have elapsed since the shaman made his public debut. Although they never all meet as a group, the ones that do participate together in various ceremonies always use time in service as a method for sorting out their position in the rank order. This organizational feature is shown in Figure 3-2. Note that the shamans are sorted by rank in each lineage, waterhole group, and hamlet. Thus, in the diagram one lineage has three shamans, the other four. When these combine into ceremonies for the waterhole group, all seven shamans are sorted into rank order from one to seven. When a hamlet ceremony is performed, all 16 shamans in the hamlet sort themselves into proper rank order.

There are reliable operational measures for determining rank in Zinacantan. The marching order in processions always places the junior man in front and the senior man in the rear. This is expressed by the Zinacantecos in terms of whether a man is *mas bankilal* or *mas 'its'inal*, "more senior" or "more junior." Similarly, there is a seating order at ritual tables when the shamans assemble to pray and eat, and this order is ordinarily followed regardless of the size of the table or the ceremony. These features are displayed in Figure 3-3.

LINKS BETWEEN CENTER AND HAMLETS

Of the approximately 2500 Zinacantecos who live in the Ceremonial Center, about one-half are permanent residents. Many of these own substantial farm lands nearby, some have small stores or work for the Mexican govern-

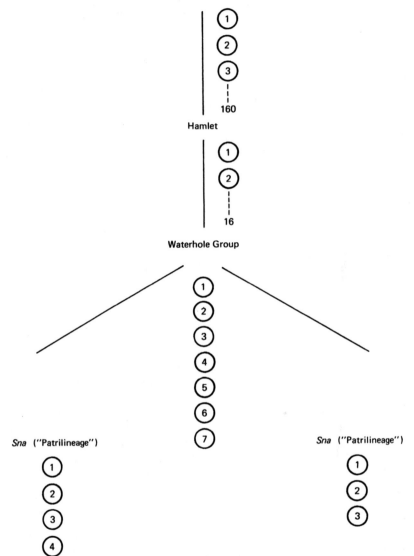

Figure 3-2. The organization of shamans in Zinacantan

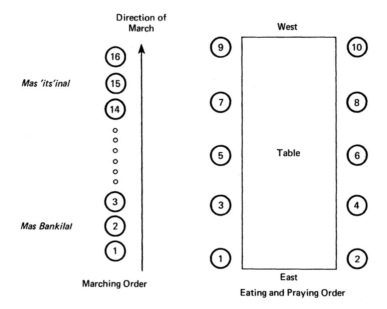

Figure 3-3. Operational measures of shaman rank

ment, and others earn their living largely by engaging in ritual activity—they are Sacristans, Musicians, or Scribes who are given food and drink in connection with ceremonies. The other people are temporary residents—the cargoholders and their families, who either own or rent houses in the Center during their year in office. These annually installed cargoholders provide a steady flow of population that moves between the hamlets and the Center. But there are other ceremonial movements that link the Center with the hamlets: the periodic flow of ritual assistants of the cargoholders into the Center bringing more maize and beans for food, wood for fires, hands to help with the ceremonies; the daily arrival of shamans with their patients to visit and pray at the mountain shrines and at the churches, as well as the arrival of assistants to collect water from the seven sacred waterholes; the arrival of large numbers of Zinacantecos—at least 8,000 to 10,000—to watch the rituals at large fiestas and to participate in the accompanying markets; the daily disputes which bring Zinacantecos to the Cabildo; and the reporting of the Principales to the Presidente each Sunday. All of these movements, and more, require the rhythmic movement of people between the hamlets in the sustaining area and the Ceremonial Center as Zinacanteco life alternates between the quiet days in the hamlets and the quickening and exciting pace in the Ceremonial Center.

4/The Social Cycle

The social structure of the Zinacantecos living in their scattered hamlets is composed of a series of units based partly upon kin ties and partly upon residential contiguity. These units, in ascending size, are: the domestic group, the *sna* (or localized lineage), and the waterhole group.

THE HOUSE COMPOUND

The basic unit of Zinacanteco social structure is the domestic group composed of kinsmen who live together in a house compound and share a single maize supply. Zinacanteco houses are of two types—an older style with wattle and daub walls and a thatched roof, and a newer style with adobe (mud brick) or cement block walls and tile roof. The tile-roofed houses last longer; even though they are more expensive to construct, they have become the most popular house.

The floor plan of both house styles is generally square, sometimes rectangular. There is seldom more than a single room per house. Windows are rare, but some houses have two doors on opposing walls. Floors are of packed earth, and cooking is done over an open fire on the floor. The smoke rises and, theoretically, flows out of spaces at the sides of the roof, but houses are often very smoky inside. The Zinacantecos sleep on reed mats on the floor, or, in some cases, on plank beds constructed in one corner of the single room. Other furniture consists of cooking equipment (see Chapter 5), a small wooden table and several small wooden chairs—about the size of children's play furniture sold in toy stores in the United States. However, the furniture is well suited for life in a small one-bedroom house. The reed sleeping mats can be rolled up and stored in a corner during the day; the small chairs take up little space and allow the men (who sit on them while women kneel or sit on the floor) to be near the warmth of the fire. House-cleaning requires little time, because muddy family feet after a rain merely add new earth to the packed earthen floor and a quick sweeping each day removes trash from the house.

Normally two or more of these houses are constructed around a central patio where women weave, men receive guests, and children play on clear, sunny days. The compound is surrounded by a fence, and off in one corner

Photo 7. Most Zinacantecos live in single-room, thatched-roof houses. Housewife in foreground is preparing to boil maize kernels in water with lime. The maize will be used to make tortillas. (Photo by Frank Cancian)

the sweat house is usually constructed. Beyond this fence is a larger plot of ground planted in maize, beans, squash, and other crops fertilized by the biweekly moving of a portable sheep corral that is shifted from place to place within the plot. During the dry season, after the maize is harvested, it is easy to look out and see the neighbors' houses, but during the rainy season, the Zinacanteco living compound is well hidden in the middle of a maize field.

Each domestic group is symbolized by the "house cross," which is erected in the patio just outside the principal house in the compound. The relationship between the domestic group and the house cross is close; a simple count of all these crosses in Zinacantan indicates the approximate total number of domestic groups living in the *municipio*. This house cross represents the smallest unit in the patriline within the patrilineage, and is the symbolic focus for the domestic group living in its compound. It mirrors the unity of this domestic group and provides a means of relating it to other parts of the social structure. The house cross is the Zinacanteco form of the household shrines found throughout the Maya area, both in contemporary communities and in the prehistoric past.

THE DEVELOPMENTAL CYCLE

The exact composition of the domestic groups varies as the unit moves through a developmental cycle and responds to economic and social pressures. But the closest economic cooperation, most of the socialization of the young, and the overwhelming majority of daily interactions occur within this domestic unit.

To understand the structure and dynamics of these domestic groups it is necessary to construct a model that takes into account what these units should be like ideally according to the Zinacanteco view, as well as the many variations observable in the municipio. One way of looking at the domestic group is to think of it as a segment of a patrilineage. The rules of patrilocal residence and patrilineal inheritance ideally construct domestic units each generation, composed of fathers and their married sons who bring their wives to live with the fathers in the same house, or in houses in the same compound. And, in fact, most traditional Zinacanteco domestic groups are patrilocal extended families living in one to three or more houses constructed around a common patio and sharing one house cross. But, at any given time, many Zinacanteco domestic units are found with different compositions, and recent data on households indicate that the incidence of single biological families, consisting of father, mother, and unmarried children, is increasing (Haviland and Haviland 1982; Collier 1989).

Another way of looking at the domestic group is as a small group of kinsmen that must contain both men and women, for each sex controls technological skills required for the successful operation of any domestic unit. To simplify the Zinacanteco view: men are required to grow and bring home the maize supply; women are required to make the tortillas. The most common arrangement is a married couple providing this union of technological specialists, and one of the important symbols of the marriage relationship is that a wife is expected to serve maize foods to her husband. But other combinations also provide maize-growers and tortilla-makers: widowed mothers with unmarried sons; widowed fathers with unmarried daughters; two old sisters, one widowed and one spinster, with an unmarried son of the widow, and so forth.

It is therefore helpful to view the domestic group in terms of a series of stages in its developmental cycle and to view the variations as reflecting the two crucial features of the system: the technological need for both sexes, and the rules of patrilocal residence and patrilineal inheritance.

When the eldest son is married, after a long and expensive courtship (see Chapter 6), he ordinarily possesses neither a house nor land of his own. Following the rule of patrilocal residence, he moves his wife into his father's house and continues to work with the father and to share the father's maize supply. No Zinacanteco really likes this arrangement; from the start he looks forward to having a house of his own, a desire that is shared by his wife, who usually has difficulties getting along with her mother-in-law. Hence he works hard to pay off the debts of his courtship and marriage, to acquire a parcel of land of his own, and to accumulate enough money to construct his own house. When he succeeds in reaching this happy state, he moves his small family to the new location, and begins to function independently and to form the nucleus for the gradual growth of a new extended family.

After a few years, the second son of the father marries, lives at first in his father's house, and later also moves into his own house. This process of fission continues until it reaches the youngest son who (because he has stayed at home, cared for the aging parents for a longer period of time, and paid for the funeral expenses of the father when he dies) inherits the father's house. Meanwhile the daughters are also marrying and moving out to live with their husband's families.

When the sons build their own houses, they ordinarily do not move very far away. If they stay in the same compound, the houses are literally next door to each other. If they move to houses on plots of land given them by the father, but further away, they are still, by our standards, close by. A move of 200 or 300 yards is regarded as a distant move by the Zinacantecos. And much cooperation in farming, herding and wood-gathering is still in order. But the families cook and eat separately, and the unit does not have the total corporate character it had when the sons were living in the same compound.

When a man's wife dies before he does, he is expected to remarry soon—in fact, the widower states (as a regular part of the funeral ceremony) whom he intends to marry while his wife's body is being carried out of the house to be taken to the cemetery. This is important to Zinacantecos, for some woman must make his tortillas.

But more frequently Zinacanteco men die before their wives do, leaving a large population of elderly widows. In these cases, the widow finds it difficult to remarry. She stays on in her husband's house, and her maize may be provided either by the youngest married son or, often, by a still unmarried son. These cases result in "remnant" domestic groups in the sense that they persist for some years as a phase near the end of the normal development cycle.

When the eldest son's sons reach marriageable age and begin to import their wives into their father's house, new patrilocal extended families are formed and persist until these new generations break off—and so the cycle is started all over again.

In actual cases a number of factors may alter this model description of the developmental cycle. Daughters sometimes marry men who have no land, and these men may be brought to live on and work lands belonging to the wives' patrilineages. Or a father may have only daughters and hence need a son-in-law in his house to help him with his farming. These situations account for the cases of matrilocal residence. Again, a tight land situation often means not only that farming land is scarce, but also that even plots for new houses are hard to acquire. Often, even though both father and son would prefer to have the son build his new house next door, the son is forced to look for a building plot further away. Quarrels within families, especially between older and younger brothers over rights to lands, may lead one of the brothers to move further away, occasionally even to another hamlet.

FUNCTIONS OF THE DOMESTIC GROUP

The major function of a Zinacanteco domestic group is reproduction and socialization of the young (see Chapter 6). There are also economic and social activities that are most effectively accomplished by cooperation among a group of kinsmen. These cooperative activities more commonly involve a group of related men or a group of related women working together on their respective tasks. Thus a group composed of a father and his sons normally forms the core of a working group for house-building, for farming maize in the lowlands, for the management of their horses and mules, and so on. A group composed of a mother, her unmarried daughters, and her daughters-in-law normally form the core of a working group for herding the sheep, cutting and fetching the wood from the hills, fetching household water, and cooking for domestic ceremonies. Furthermore, there is much sharing of utensils, tools, and ritual equipment within the group. For example, if one of the houses does not have the proper gourd containers or all four colors of maize required for a curing ceremony, these items are easily borrowed from another house in the compound. Finally, the domestic group is the crucial structural unit that provides the necessary people for all the roles to be filled in domestic ceremonies. The shaman may have to be imported if none of the men in the group is a curer. But all of the ritual assistants, as well as the women who do the cooking for the ceremonies, are usually selected from the domestic group. And all of the members of the group attend the ceremonies, such as curing, house dedication, baptism, and so on.

RELATIONSHIPS AMONG KINSMEN*

Structurally, the most crucial relationships are between a father and his sons, and between brothers. They are all members of the same patrilineage and they form a core of relationships for the control and inheritance of lands and houses and for the exercise of jural authority in the system. But the relationship between mother-in-law and daughters-in-law is also important, especially since they are left alone to manage the house, the children, and the sheep while the men are away farming in the lowlands. The relationship between a father and his sons is normally warm and close, but there is considerable strain between older and younger brothers, especially when there are arguments over inheritance and control of land. The mother-daughter relationship is likewise warm and close, and married daughters frequently run home to their mothers, especially in the early years of marriage. When this happens, the daughter's husband must make an appearance with a bottle of liquor, present it to his parents-in-law, and give long explanations and reassurances that his wife will be provided better treatment at his father's house before the wife and her parents are persuaded that she should return. On the other hand, the mother-in-law's relationship with daughters-in-law is predictably one of stress. The daughter-in-law is under pressure to perform well in a new situation for which she has been given little preparation. While sons spend most of their lives working under their father's supervision, and are trained from birth to respond to the father's orders, the daughters move away at marriage. They come to know the mother-in-law slightly, if at all, before the wedding takes place. A daughter must spend most of her life working under conditions in which an older woman who is not her mother initiates action and gives the orders for daily tasks.

KINSHIP

The kin terms used in Zinacantan are displayed in Figures 4-1, 4-2, and 4-3; Table 4-1 presents a complete list of these terms and their ranges of application to genealogical positions in the kinship system. These are "reference terms" in contrast to "address terms" (which are described below). By "reference terms" we mean the kin terms that Zinacantecos utilize in Tzotzil in referring to specified relatives while talking to a third person. In other words, the terms represent the response in the sentence frame: "He is my _____ ."

The terms for lineal relatives are presented in Figure 4-1. Note that all siblings are distinguished according to sex, sex of speaker, and relative age, except the dyad "Elder Sister"—"Younger Sibling," where one term is applied to each member; that children (regardless of sex) are referred to by one

---

* This discussion of relationships among kinsmen utilizes some terms that may be unfamiliar to beginning students. All such terms are defined in the glossary.

TABLE 4-1   ZINACANTECO KIN TERMS

Term	Range of Application
htot	Fa
hme'	Mo
hmuk'tatot	FaFa, MoFa; variant for FaBr, FaSiHu, MoSiHu, Male Cousin older than ego.
hmuk'tot	Variant for FaFa, MoFa
hmuk'tame'	MoMo, FaMo; variant for MoSi, FaSi, MoBrWi, FaBrWi, Female Cousin older than ego.
h-huntot	FaBr, MoBr, FaSiHu, MoSiHu, Male Cousin older than ego.
h-hunme'	MoSi, FaSi, MoBrWi, FaBrWi, Female Cousin older than ego.
hbankil	ElBr (male speaking)
hshibnel	ElBr (female speaking)
hvish	ElSi
kits'in	YoBr (male speaking)
kishlel	YoSi (male speaking)
hmuk	Younger sibling (female speaking)
hch'amal	Child (male speaking)
kol	Child (female speaking)
hmom	Grandchild
h-hunch'amal	Cousin younger than ego (male speaking)
h-hunnich'on	Variant for cousin younger than ego (male speaking)
h-hun'ol	Cousin younger than ego (female speaking)
kahnil	Wi
hmalal	Hu
hni'	DaHu
hni'mol	WiFa
hni'me'el	WiMo
kalib	SoWi
kalib mol	HuFa
kalib me'el	HuMo
hbol	WiBr or SiHu (male speaking)
h-havan	HuSi or BrWi (female speaking)
hmu'	WiSi or BrWi (male speaking), HuBr or SiHu (female speaking)
hni'al	Child's Spouse's Parents

term by male speakers, another by female speakers; and that only one term is used for grandchildren. A variant term—*hmuk'tot*—is used in the western part of the municipio; otherwise there was complete consistency in these terms for lineal relatives in the sample of twenty-five genealogies collected by Jane F. Collier (1967).

The terms for collateral relatives are displayed in Figure 4-2, which has been simplified by including only father's sister and mother's brother and their spouses; hence the system is clearly "bilateral." The figure is further simplified by placing all cousins older than ego to the left and all cousins younger than ego to the right of the chart. In addition, brother's children are joined with sister's children because no distinction is made between them.

Unlike the more stable terms for lineal relatives, the kin terms for col-

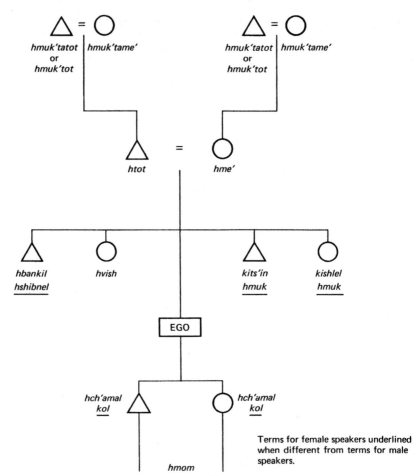

Figure 4-1. Kin terms for lineal relatives (adapted from Jane F. Collier 1967)

lateral relatives are obviously undergoing change. In the twenty-five genealogies there was great variation among the informants. The more traditional
system is contained in the first alternatives in each case; the most important
variant terms are found in the second alternatives in Figure 3-2. Thus, for
example, a father's sister was traditionally referred to as *h-hunme'*, but is
now commonly referred to as *hmuk'tame'*.

On the other hand, the terms presented in Figure 4-3 form a core of
consistent and stable terms, covering the most important affinal relationships.

An examination of the terms for consanguineal relatives (both lineal and
collateral) reveals that five distinct variables characterize the more traditional
pattern. These variables are (1) generation, (2) lineal or collateral, (3) age
relative to *ego*, (4) sex of referent, and (5) sex of speaker. The traditional
pattern can be neatly diagrammed as shown below (from Jane F. Collier 1967).

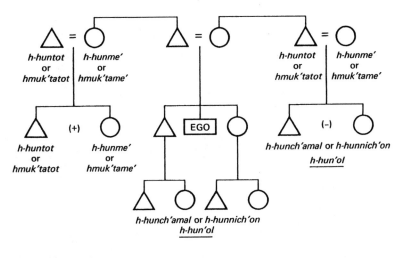

Figure 4-2. Kin terms for collateral relatives (adapted from Jane F. Collier 1967)

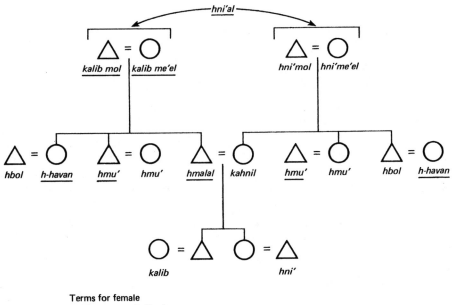

Figure 4-3. Affinal terms (adapted from Jane F. Collier 1967)

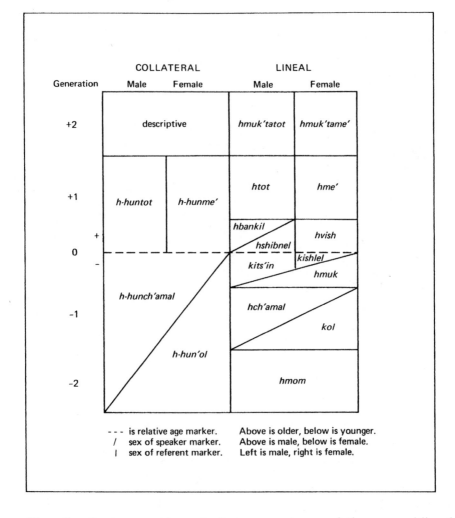

Note that the two most important components are relative age and lineal vs. collateral. Relative age divides the whole system in two, even extending to ego's generation as ego differentiates between older and younger siblings. The lineal vs. collateral division would be even neater if we add the terms *hmuk'ta huntot* and *hmuk'ta hunme'* to the upper left hand corner. Then the diagram would be completely consistent with all the collateral terms containing the root *hun* and neatly divided from ego's own bilateral line. Jane Collier thinks "it is probably safe to assume that this pattern was in use two generations ago" (1967).

Note also in the diagram that the sex of referent division is always made for relatives older than ego, but seldom made for younger relatives. The younger relatives are typically distinguished by sex of speaker rather than by sex of the referent.

Address terms, except in special cases determined by the *compadrazgo* and other ritual relationships, follow a simple rule: an older kinsman is called *tot* or *me'* (depending on sex), and responds by calling the younger person by name. Non-kin, in contrast are addressed as *totik* or *me'tik*, or less formally, both kin and non-kin may be addressed as "*tot*" _____ (plus name or title), or "*me*"_____ (plus name or title)" depending on sex (Michelle Rosaldo 1967).

While descent in Zinacantan, represented by the inheritance of the double surname (see below), is wholly patrilineal, and inheritance (with an ideal of equal distribution among sons) of land and house sites tends to be patrilineal, the localized patrilineages are shallow, seldom exceeding three generations in depth. This poses a contrast to San Pablo Chalchihuitán, a more isolated Tzotzil municipio north of Zinacantan, which still preserves a unilineal Omaha-type kinship system. In Zinacantan, a residential arrangement, which is essentially an ego-specific (rather than a lineage) alliance, seems to be implicit in the terminology (Michelle Rosaldo 1967). I mean by this statement that the kin terms reflect patterns of behavior geared more to sets of dyadic relationships between pairs of kinsmen than to alliances among lineages. Whether or not Zinacantan once had an Omaha-type system is not known. What is important now are sets of reciprocal relationships that classify kinsmen and designate the appropriate role behavior among them in residential domestic groups.

The reciprocal dyadic relationships assume three forms. In the first form the same term is used reciprocally by two persons standing in symmetrical relationship to each other. A good example is the term *hni'al*, meaning "child's spouse's parents," which is used reciprocally between the parents of a married couple, and represents the alliance between the domestic groups involved. In the second form reciprocity occurs when the same term covers two kin types that are reciprocal. An example is found in the terms for brothers-in-law and sisters-in-law in the terminology for affinal relatives. A third form occurs in cases when two terms are reciprocals of each other—as, for example, in the pair *hmuk'tatot—hch'amal* ("grandfather"—"grandchild," male speaking).

The reciprocal relationships between ascending and descending generations are of further significance in that the ascending generations are divided by sex (into "grandfathers" and "grandmothers") whereas the descending generations are differentiated by sex of the speaker (with grandfather and grandmother each using separate terms to designate "grandchild").

In ego's generation relative age is of overriding importance with male ego making both a distinction between older and younger brother, and between older and younger sister. On the other hand, a female ego differentiates between older siblings by age, but groups her younger siblings together. These differences are congruent with the importance of rank among siblings, especially brothers, to the male Zinacanteco, who has constructed a symbolic world that places great emphasis upon "junior-senior." They are also congruent with the fact that a female ego is less concerned with rank and, perhaps more importantly, that she serves (in the years before her marriage) as a substitute mother for her younger siblings. In this respect, the pair of terms *hvish—hmuk* ("older sister"—"younger sibling") parallels the set *hme'-kol* ("mother"—"female's child"). For as the mother cares for her children, the older sister cares for her younger siblings.

This affinal terminology expresses not only the alliance between the two domestic groups in the reciprocal term used between the parents of the married couple, but also differentiates clearly between husband's ascending kinsmen and wife's ascending kinsmen in the two terms *kalib* and *hni'*, respectively. Note that the same terms are applied to son's wife and to daughter's husband, making the system consistent with respect to the alliance between the two lineages. We have been unable to translate *hni'*, but *kalib* has a common derivation with the verb *-alah*, meaning "to give birth," in which case "son's wife" is appropriately defined as a woman brought into the lineage to give birth to children.

It should be noted that many of these more traditional kin terms are being replaced in everyday usage by compadrazgo terms (see Chapter 6) and that there is a marked trend in the direction of using descriptive terms for collateral relatives. Younger Zinacantecos are more likely to refer to aunts and uncles, nieces and nephews, and cousins with descriptive terms; that is, instead of referring to an uncle as *h-huntot*, they are more likely to designate him as "My father's older brother." While the lineal and affinal terms are being preserved, the collateral terms are in a rapid state of change.

DAILY LIFE IN THE DOMESTIC GROUP

A typical day in a traditional Zinacanteco household begins before dawn, when the woman awakens, gently blows the smoldering embers in the hearth into a fire, and starts grinding maize for the day's tortillas (see Chapter 5 for details on the process of tortilla making). The daughters and daughters-in-law help her with the early morning tasks, bringing wood for the fire, boiling a pot of beans, grinding maize on a second *metate*, or patting out tortillas. The recent introduction of corn grinding mills in Zinacantan has shortened the time needed for the grinding process, but the women still awaken first and start the household fires.

Although the whole household is awake by sunrise, the men and small children may linger on their *petates* (reed mats) or in their plank beds, for they have no such urgent chores during the early morning hours. The men may attend to their horses or mules, look over the crops growing in their compound, or watch the sunrise. But the air is chilly, and soon they gather around the fire to warm themselves and to visit leisurely. By seven or eight, enough tortillas have been made to start the morning meal. The men, seated in a semi-circle of tiny chairs, accept a gourdful of water from a kneeling woman and rinse their hands and mouths. The woman then presents them with tortillas, beans or greens, and sweetened coffee, always announcing each food as she places it before them. A tiny dish of salt is always set down after the food, and each man sprinkles a little on his beans or greens before he takes a bite. Torn pieces of tortillas are used to scoop up the beans or handle the hot greens, and the women replenish the supply throughout the meal by expertly tossing freshly cooked tortillas into the gourd container at the man's feet. When the men have finished, they hand each container back to the women, who finish any bits of food the men may have left. The women nibble as they cook and finish their informal "meals" after the men have left, for they, in contrast to the men, tend to see food as a continuous stream of tidbits throughout the day.

After breakfast the men, if they are working at home, may cultivate the maize, beans, or squash in their compound, repair a fence, or perhaps go to Zinacantan Center to perform some political or ritual task.

One of the women or girls lets the sheep out of the corral and leads them out to graze, taking her backstrap loom along so she can keep busy weaving while she watches the sheep on a nearby hillside. Other women and young girls either go to the waterhole to wash clothes and fetch water for household use, or set off to find firewood. At the waterhole, they may spend the morning rubbing the wet clothes on smooth stones, later laying them out to dry on rocks, bushes, or the ground near their house. When they return, each woman is bent forward under the weight of her waterjug, which a tumpline across her forehead supports and keeps in place on her back.

Every few days, the household supply of firewood must be replenished. The women and girls arm themselves with billhooks, machetes, and ropes and walk over trails and rock-strewn *milpas* to a wooded field, perhaps an hour and a half away. Here the group scatters and each woman or girl finds young trees to cut down or large broken branches to split for firewood. When the pieces are cut, split lengthwise, stripped of bark, and fashioned into an appropriate length, each worker carefully piles her pieces together, binds them with a rope and attaches her tumpline. She then hoists her heavy load onto her back with the help of a friend, adjusts the tumpline on her forehead, and the single file of barefoot women begins the hike back home, perhaps stopping along the path to gather a few greens for the mid-day meal.

A nursing baby always accompanies its mother on water and wood trips, either jogging along on her back supported by a large cloth she ties in front, or, if the baby is older, sitting astride the waterjug or pile of wood that the mother is carrying. After being weaned, however, small children are held and entertained by slightly older sisters who may not yet be strong enough to carry heavy loads of water or wood.

At noon the men and women reassemble for the midday meal, unless of course the men have been working in the lowlands, or are too far away to come back to eat. Both menu and procedure are similar to the morning meal, with men being formally served as they sit on their tiny chairs, and the kneeling women nibbling on bits of food as they prepare it.

During the afternoon, the men and grown boys continue the morning's planting, hoeing, and other work in the fields or around the house. Their wives and sisters are more likely to do less strenuous tasks than they did in the morning—weaving, cooking, caring for the children, or simply chatting with each other. At sundown, the third meal of the day is served, and is followed by a period of quiet visiting around the hearth. By about 8 p.m., the family has normally gone to sleep, to recharge their energies for another strenuous day that will begin before the sun comes up again.

THE *SNA*

Zinacanteco domestic groups are embedded in two other crucial social units—the localized lineage (or *sna*) and the waterhole group—which in turn are grouped into the hamlets. Tzotzil has no generic name for either the small domestic group, described in the last section, or for the larger grouping of domestic units, even though both are crucial elements of the social structure. These two types of units may be talked about only as specific groupings of relatives in particular contexts, never as general, abstract concepts. *Sna*, for example, means "the house of." A Zinacanteco who hears of *Sna' Akovetik* ("the Houses of Wasp Nests") can judge from the context that a collection of domestic groups or families making up a localized lineage unit is being discussed. A single domestic unit within the Wasp Nests might be called, for example, *Sna Shun' Akov*, "the house of John Wasp Nest." I have adopted the Tzotzil word *sna* to refer in the abstract to the larger unit—that is, the unit composed of one or more localized patrilineages that are extensions of the patrilocally extended groups described in the last chapter. Genealogical connections can be traced in these localized patrilineages, but they reach back no more than about four generations. The members of such a patrilineage live on adjacent lands they have inherited from their ancestors. The unit possesses some jural authority in that important decisions for its members are made by the most senior men. Some patrilineages also own important ritual paraphernalia which they keep in their houses and regularly allow on request to be transported to the Ceremonial Center for special ceremonies (see Chapter 7).

The *sna* takes its name from the localized patrilineages. If the *sna* contains only one lineage, the unit is simply called by the name of that lineage—for example *Sna' Akovetik*. If the *sna* is larger and contains two or more lineages, it takes its name from the predominant lineage which was the first to settle on the lands which are now controlled by the *sna*. Thus, *Sna 'Ok'iletik*, "the Houses of the Coyotes" in the hamlet of Paste', contains not only the coyote lineage, but also two smaller lineages that have settled next to the coyotes and have intermarried with them.

The *snas* vary in size from those containing one localized patrilineage, only four houses, and less than fifteen people to very large ones with thirteen patrilineages and over 150 people living in more than forty houses. But whatever the history and number of lineages in a *sna*, its present composition and boundaries are made operationally clear by the *K'in Krus* ceremony performed each May and each October for the Ancestral Gods and the Earth Owner. *K'in* is a Tzotzil word that means "fiesta" to the Zinacantecos, but significantly it is derived from an ancient Maya word that means "Sun," "Day," "Time." It is therefore the "Day" or "Time" of the "Cross."

Each *sna* maintains a series of cross shrines. Some are erected on nearby mountains and designated as *Kalvaryos*, which defines them as means of communication with the assembled ancestral deities of the lineages making up the *sna*. Others are erected in caves and defined as means of communication with the Earth Owner. All of the shamans who live in the *sna* assemble in rank order to perform the ritual for the *K'in Krus* ceremony. If a small *sna* does not have a shaman, it must import one from a neighboring *sna*.

The *K'in Krus* ceremony has four basic parts. First, a formal ritual meal is eaten in the house of the outgoing Senior Mayordomo, who is designated each year and serves as the host for the ceremony. The expenses of the food, liquor, candles, and fireworks are shared by the Junior Mayordomo and by the heads of the various domestic groups, among whom a cash collection is taken up in advance. Seated at the ritual table in rank order are the senior male members of the predominant lineage of the *sna*; then come the shamans and the four Mayordomos—the two leaving office and the two coming into office the following year. Chicken is always served, and the meal is accompanied by three rounds of rum liquor. Second, a long prayer is recited over the candles and flowers that will be offered by the shamans, who pray in rank order holding censers with burning copal incense. They pray in such phrases as these:

> In the divine name of Jesus Christ my Lord
> > How much my father
> > How much my lord,
> > > My lowly earth has come
> > > My lowly mud has come (that is, I am in your presence)
>
> With this we beseech divine pardon
> With this we beg divine permission
> > At your holy side
> > At your holy front
> > > Holy ancestral gods
> > > Holy angels
> > > Holy priests
> > > Holy earth lords
> > > Will you accept from me
> > > Will you receive from me
> > This lowly little bit, then
> > This humble amount, then
> > > We shall prepare, then
> > > We shall place them, then
> > > > Our humble pine branches
> > > > Our humble candles.

Other participants then come to the foot of the table to recite prayers. Third, an all-night ceremonial circuit proceeds counter-clockwise around the lands belonging to the *sna*, and stops are made at all the cross shrines, which are decorated with fresh pinetree tops and red geraniums, to offer violin, harp, and guitar music, candles, liquor, incense, and prayers to the ancestors of the *sna* and to the Earth Owner. The ceremony ends the following morning back at the house of the Senior Mayordomo with a closing ritual meal.

This ceremony occurs near the time of the Day of the Holy Cross in May (officially May 3 in the Catholic calendar). But since it is repeated at the end of the rainy season in October, it appears to have little to do with the Christian concept of the cross. Christ and the crucifixion are not mentioned. Rather, the ceremonial circuit appears to be a symbolic expression of the rights the *sna* members have to the lands they have inherited from their patrilineal ancestors. The rituals for these ancestral patrons not only pay respect to these deities, but also link together the descendants as common worshippers and members of the same *sna*. In this way the ceremony symbolizes the unity of the *sna* as a structurally significant unit of Zinacanteco society.

PATRONYMICS IN ZINACANTAN

Beyond about four generations the precise names of ancestors are forgotten, and exact genealogical connections can no longer be traced. There survives, however, an important system of patronymics that is still functionally important in Zinacanteco society.

Each Zinacanteco possesses three names: (1) a first name, such as *Romin* (Tzotzil for *Domingo*) or *Maruch* (Tzotzil for *Maria*); (2) a so-called Spanish surname, such as *Krus* (Tzotzil for *de la Cruz*); and (3) an Indian surname, such as *'Ok'il* ("Coyote"). Both of the surnames are inherited patrilineally and retained throughout life, even by women after they are married and living patrilocally. The first name is given a child at the baptismal ceremony. The Indian surnames combine with the Spanish surnames in a system in which a specified group of Indian names combine with one particular Spanish name. Zinacantan has some seventy Indian surnames that combine with sixteen Spanish surnames.

A given person might be named *Romin Peres Tanhol*, but since the Indian name *Tanhol* ("lime head") can combine only with the Spanish name *Peres* (derived from *Perez*), he may be identified simply as *Romin Tanhol*.

The Zinacantecos now utilize a very limited set of personal first names—twenty-seven for men, sixteen for women. Some are much more common than others. Favored men's names include Marian, Romin, Petul, Antun; the favored women's names include Maruch, Pashku, Matal, and Shunka.

With 20,000 Indians now living in Zinacantan, the total list of first names and surnames is very limited for differentiating so many people, and the problem of maintaining an accurate census, or even keeping track of individuals, is formidable. One *sna* I know has seventeen men all named *Marian*

Lopis Ch'iku, and in a few cases the men are full brothers living in the same domestic group. The Zinacantecos themselves have difficulties differentiating people, and use of kin terms does not identify well enough for them. Thus, there is a proliferation of nicknames, never used in direct address, but nearly always used for reference. For example, a man with a squash-shaped head may be called "Squash," while a guitar-player might be labelled "Guitar" in Tzotzil.

The meaning and significance of the Spanish surnames is obscure, since they appear to have lost whatever functions they may once have had. It may be they are vestiges of larger patrilineal units, possibly phratries.

The Indian surnames are, however, still functionally important designations of exogamous units which I shall call "patriclans." There is a strong rule that one may never marry a person of the same Indian surname, even those close genealogical connections have been lost. This means that while a man can marry some classes of close relatives (from our point of view), other more distant classes are prohibited. Thus, a Zinacanteco may, and sometimes does, marry a mother's sister or more frequently a mother's sister's daughter or a mother's brother's daughter, but he may never marry a father's sister or a father's brother's daughter, because these women possess his Indian surname and are hence members of his own patriclan.

THE WATERHOLE GROUP

The next unit of ascending size in Zinacanteco social structure is what I have chosen to call the "waterhole group." Again, this group does not have a generic name in Tzotzil, but a particular waterhole group can be described by reference to the name of the waterhole around which the group lives.

Waterhole groups vary in size from two to thirteen *snas*, depending largely upon the amount of water available for household use and for watering livestock. The availability of water varies seasonally. During the summer rainy season the larger waterholes contain an ample supply and the smaller ones have enough to support many households. But in the winter dry season, many of the smaller waterholes dry up completely, so that more households have to depend upon fewer sources of water. This seasonal cycle in the availability of water leads to a corresponding cycle in the size of many of the waterhole groups. During the dry season there are fewer larger groups drawing water from the major waterholes, and during the rainy season more smaller groups draw water from many more waterholes closer to their houses. For example, in the paraje of *'Apas* there are eight waterhole groups drawing water from eight waterholes in the rainy season; in the dry season the same households regroup into four large waterhole groups, drawing water from the four major waterholes that contain water the year around.

The major waterholes have multiple openings: one for household water; one for washing clothes; and one for supplying water for the livestock. Some maintain water in all the openings, even at the height of the dry season, but others retain water in only one portion, thus forcing their users to draw water for all three purposes from a single opening.

The waterholes are highly sacred, and myths are told about each of them describing the circumstances under which the ancestors found the water and the way in which the waterhole acquired its distinctive name. The following myth, for example, is told about "Little Waterhole" in the Paraje of Paste':

> There went a man, he went looking for soap-root, in the mountains, by "Little Water." He went to look at "Little Water." There, he heard a music-band, and so he went to see, he went to see what he heard, where the music was. But suddenly, it started to rain. Not knowing if the rain would go on, he went to sleep at the foot of a tree; he waited for the rain to pass. A thunderbolt came, and the man was hit by the bolt. The thunder passed, but the tree was destroyed; where it was standing, the thunder has passed. Still, the music was playing, and the man heard where it was. He went to see where it was, and then he saw that there was water. It was a very small well.
>
> When he saw it, he returned home. "There is a well," he said. "Where?" the others asked. "Over there, let's go see it," he said. They went to look at the water, but it wasn't little, it was a big well. They saw how big it was and were frightened and cornets played at them. There was a cave there, and they went in, into the ground. Then he returned home. "Well, I only speak now so you know where the water is. I am going to die," the man said. "There I remained, one with the ground, there, in the ground," he said. In three days the man died. He said just before he died, "You can drink the water, I will look over it, but you mustn't lose its name, it is 'Little Water.' "

Each waterhole group maintains a series of cross shrines for its waterhole. One of these shrines is at the side of the waterhole; another is on a mountain or hill above the waterhole and is designated as the *Kalvaryo* for the whole waterhole group. At this *Kalvaryo* the waterhole group's ancestors are believed to assemble and hold meetings to survey the affairs of their descendants and to wait for the semi-annual offerings in the *K'in Krus* ceremony for the waterhole. This ceremony ordinarily precedes by a few days the various *K'in Krus* ceremonies for the *snas* that comprise the waterhole group.

The ceremony for the waterhole is performed by all of the shamans that live in the waterhole group. It follows the same pattern as the ceremonies for the *snas*, except that before the opening ritual meal, the men assemble to clean out the waterhole, repair fences around the openings, and fix up the cross shrines. During the ceremonial circuit, ritual is performed at the waterhole, at the houses of the Mayordomos, and at the *Kalvaryo* where the ancestors are waiting for their gifts.

The ceremony appears to express the rights that members of the waterhole group have to draw water from their waterhole and their obligations to care for it properly. Control of rights to water is crucial for human and animal life in the Chiapas Highlands, especially during the long dry season from October to May when supplies of water are strictly limited. Just as the *K'in Krus* for the *sna* expresses rights in land, so the *K'in Krus* for the waterhole group expresses rights in water. By including rituals for the deities associated with the waterhole, the ceremony links together all the *snas* that compose a waterhole group, and hence symbolizes the unity of the waterhole group as another structurally significant unit in Zinacanteco society.

The waterhole group also holds some jural authority. Men who refuse to contribute to the expenses of the semiannual ceremonies or to the labor needed for cleaning out the waterhole may be fined by the shamans or even excluded from using the waterhole.

The next unit of ascending size in the social structure, and the largest subdivision of the total municipio, is the hamlet, the organization of which was described in Chapter 3.

Although I have described domestic groups, *snas*, and waterhole groups as if they were the same throughout the municipio, there is, in fact, considerable variation in the details of social and cultural behavior in different hamlets. Each hamlet tends to be both geographically and socially isolated. For the main lines of communication among Zinacantecos from different hamlets occur not within the hamlets but in the Ceremonial Center and in the market in San Cristobal. For this reason both market behavior and ritual behavior occurring in the Ceremonial Center are constantly standardized. But the patterns of behavior and belief that are activated mainly at the hamlet level display more variation. For example, in the well-watered valley in which the hamlet of Nabenchauk is located, most *snas* have their own waterholes rather than sharing them with others in waterhole groups. In various hamlets waterlines bringing water from mountain springs have been installed with the aid of the Mexican government in recent years. As a result, household water is now carried from the closest faucet on the pipeline rather than from distant waterholes. In the hamlet of 'Apas, the house cross is pulled up and placed against the patio fence when a member of the domestic group dies and the funeral begins; also, the graves in the cemetery are roofed over with small board roofs to provide "houses" for the dead. These two customs are unique to this hamlet.

One of the principal reasons why each hamlet is so socially isolated is that each tends to be a strongly endogamous unit. When a Zinacanteco seeks a mate, he must not marry: (1) his mother; (2) a *comadre* (see Chapter 6); or (3) a girl with the same Indian surname. Any other woman in Zinacantan is theoretically a potential spouse, but in point of fact men seek spouses as close to home as the three incest rules permit. For example, in Paste', where I collected precise data on the married couples in the hamlet, almost 50 percent of the wives were reared in the same waterhole group as their husbands; another 30 percent were reared in different waterhole groups but within the hamlet. Almost all of the remaining 20 percent of marriages involved spouses drawn from the two closest neighboring hamlets.

5/The Economic Cycle

The Mayas have been maize cultivators *par excellence* for some 4500 years, and the Zinacantecos are no exception. Not only does the overwhelming bulk of daily calories come from maize, but a proper meal without maize in some form is inconceivable to them. They are aware that some other people, such as anthropologists, serve meals without maize. But a Zinacanteco hostess would not dream of serving a "civilized" meal without tortillas, whatever else she might be serving. And Zinacanteco men, who spend long periods away from home working their fields in the Lowlands, invariably take maize foods with them—either the maize dough to mix in a gourd of water for the trail or for midday nourishment in the fields or toasted tortillas for their morning and evening meals.

Maize, like humans, is believed to have an "inner soul," which is found in the ear and in the "heart" of each kernel just as it is found in the "heart" of a person. Maize is often referred to by terms that translate as "the sunbeams of the gods." It follows that maize is handled with extreme care; kernels that drop on the ground are carefully picked up, and great care is exercised to avoid spilling the corn gruel, *atole*.

Although maize is the focus of their food-producing activities, Zinacantecos grow, gather, buy, and consume a variety of other foods. They cultivate not only beans and squashes (those other members of the important trinity of aboriginal Mesoamerican food crops), but also chiles, chayotes, and fruit trees such as peach and apple. They keep and eat chickens and pigs, and gather a variety of wild plants and animals for food. In markets they purchase fish and fruits from the Lowlands, as well as beef, rum liquor, coffee, sugar, and wheat bread, especially for ritual occasions. The principal condiment is salt, served with every meal and considered important both for nourishment and for ritual protection.

THE MAIZE CYCLE

The annual agricultural cycle for the production of maize is well adjusted to the winter dry season-summer rainy season climatic pattern of southern Mexico. The fields are prepared for planting in the late winter and spring (when the brush and/or stubble can be burned); the main planting occurs either just before or during the onset of the summer rains in May. The maize grows and matures during the rainy season and is harvested and transported home after the dry season sets in again. Once the maize is safely stored away in the granaries, it is available for processing into the various types of corn foods consumed by the Zinacantecos.

Zinacantecos cultivate maize on three types of land that are differently controlled and differently situated geographically: (1) small plots of land owned individually by men and located near their homes in the Highlands; (2) plots of *ejido* land, ordinarily 4 hectares,* some located in the Highlands, but more often located in *ejido* holdings at lower elevations; and (3) larger plots of land rented from Ladino landowners in the Lowlands along both banks of the Grijalva River (see Frank Cancian 1972; George Collier 1975; Price 1968).

The farming operations in the Highlands are relatively small-scale, many of them almost like garden plots that the Zinacantecos have inherited from their fathers. Since the plots are small and the yield is not great (compared to farming the Lowlands), an interesting system of fertilization is employed to increase production. The portable sheep corral is moved about every two weeks within the parcel so that the manure will add fertility to the soil. But even with this measure, most Zinacanteco families could never subsist on the limited amount of maize produced on these small plots.

Considerably more maize is currently grown on the 12,070 hectares of *ejido* land the Zinacantecos acquired in the 1940s as part of the program of agrarian reform of the Mexican government. These 4 hectare parcels are assigned to heads of households by an ejido committee composed of Zinacantecos. The ejido member who receives rights to land may use the plot during his lifetime, and one of his sons may inherit the rights. The parcel may never be divided nor sold; and in case it goes unused, it may be reassigned to another individual by the committee.

Even more maize is cultivated on rented lands in the Lowlands in the valley of the Grijalva River south of Zinacantan. On a clear day a Zinacanteco can stand on the rim of the escarpment and see all the way to his fields along the banks of the river. But the land lies more than 5000 feet below him and at least a hard six hours' walk or a long, two- to three-hour truck ride away. These lands are rented by groups of patrilineally related men (occasionally by unrelated men) who band together under the leadership of a *responsable*, one of their kinsmen who knows enough Spanish to deal with the Ladino landowners. He makes the rental agreement with the landowner, and is responsible to see that the group pays the rent in the fall, for the landowner does not collect from each individual but from the group as a whole. The rent is usually fixed as two *fanegas* (a *fanega* is 180 metric liters) of maize for every *almud* (15 metric liters) of maize seed planted by the Indian renter. This system of fixed rent places all the risk on the Zinacantecos.

Once rental arrangements have been made, the fields of the renting group

---

* A hectare is a unit of land measuring 100 by 100 meters or 10,000 square meters.

Photo 8. A Zinacanteco in his maize field. (Photo by Frank Cancian)

are laid out in such a way as to give each man an equal part, both in quality and in quantity of land.

The technology used in Zinacanteco farming is still fundamentally aboriginal in character. While they utilize a few steel tools—axes, machetes, billhooks, and hoes—the farming techniques are those of swidden agriculture perfected centuries ago. The pattern is one of cutting down the trees and brush, burning them when dry, and then planting with a pointed digging stick. Fields are planted for varying periods of time, depending upon elevation and quality of the soil, and then allowed to grow into brush again. In the Highlands, where fertilization is practiced, the cycle is long. In the Lowlands, the cycle is much shorter; the parcels can be farmed for only three years, and then the fields must be moved, allowing the old parcels several years to lie fallow.

In the small Highland plots, the corn stubble is cut, raked into piles, and burned. The topsoil is then turned over with a hoe, which works the sheep manure into the soil and prepares the ground for planting.

In the Lowlands the fields are prepared either by burning the stubble, in the case of an old field, or by cutting, drying, and burning the trees and brush of the new fields. Cutting is done between December and March and the burning takes place in April, just before the onset of the rains.

In the Highlands maize is planted in March, but in the Lowlands, where the temperatures are higher, the planting is not done until the rains begin in May. Planting is considered a much more delicate task than preparing the fields, and is accompanied by extensive ritual activity. The planting in the large fields in the Lowlands is always preceded by a ceremony in which candles, incense, liquor, and prayers by a shaman are offered to the Earth Owner, the ruler and sender of the clouds, rain, and wind. The ceremonial circuit includes the corners and center of the cornfield, and the prayers emphasize rain-making.

The planting is done by making a hole in the soil with a planting stick. The carefully selected seed is carried in a shoulder bag. The planter drapes the bag of seed over his left shoulder and works with the planting stick in his right hand. He makes a hole about 3 inches deep with the stick, then reaches into the bag for six grains of maize and drops them into the hole with his left hand. He then covers up the hole using either his feet or the digging stick. Re-seeding, if necessary, is done about two weeks later.

The number of times a field must be weeded during the growing season varies. A new field is weeded only once, if it has been made in heavy brush where large trees were felled and dense weeds have not yet grown up; other fields are weeded at least twice, once in June and once in July. The first weeding, preceded by another ceremony, begins about mid-June in the Lowlands and is the longest and most difficult of all the farming operations. It takes a man about twelve to fifteen days of hard labor to weed a hectare plot. The second weeding begins about mid-July and ordinarily takes less time since the weeds do not appear as vigorously after the first hoeing.

The weeding is done with a hoe, which each man owns and carries with him in his net bag when traveling to the Lowlands. The handle is cut in the fields and left in the Lowlands when the metal hoe is brought home for safekeeping. In weeding, the men always work barefooted, proceeding from left to right across the field, and uphill, because this means less bending of the back. The working group always hoes together. Work begins shortly after dawn; there is a stop for *pozol* (maize dough mixed with water) about 9 a.m., and a meal at noon. They continue until about 4 p.m. when they stop to rest, look after their horses and mules, and gather wild plants to supplement the evening meal of toasted tortillas and beans.

In recent years the Zinacantecos have begun to spray chemical weed killers on their fields, a practice that is now largely replacing hoeing as the principal method of weed control.

In September, when the maize is ripe, the Zinacanteco farmers return again to their lowland fields to bend the cornstalks. The stalks are broken just above the middle, and the top halves are bent down almost to the ground, leaving the full ears to harden on the stalks. This process serves three purposes: it cuts off the food supply so that maize begins to dry; it prevents the rain from rotting the ears of maize; and it gives beans planted at this time more sun so they will grow between the rows of maize.

In the Highlands, maize is harvested in October, but in the Lowlands, harvesting begins in November and continues into December and January. The Zinacantecos harvest the corn using a deer antler corn-husker about 4 inches long. It is carried on a cord tied to their belts. The sharp end is inserted through the ends of the husks and pulled upward, thus starting the separation. The husks are peeled down the sides, using both hands at once. The ear is then removed with a sharp twist, leaving the husks on the stalks. The ears are placed in bags and carried to the threshing area where the shelling is done by one of two methods: (1) the ears are placed in a net bag with holes of a size that allow the kernels, but not the cobs, to come out as the bag of corn is pounded with a pole; (2) a platform is constructed and a net of cowhide stretched parallel to the ground underneath so that the kernels fall to the ground while the cobs stay in the net when the ears are pounded with a pole on the platform.

The shelled maize is heaped in piles, and the landlord comes for his rent. Now the Zinacantecos can calculate how good the year has been. They have tried their utmost by reseeding to be certain that each clump of maize had at least three or four stalks, and they have provided all the necessary weeding operations and the necessary ceremonies for the Earth Owner to keep the proper amount of rain falling. If an average of 5 ears grew in each hill of stalks and the ears grew to ample size, the year was a good one and they should have more than an average of 8 *fanegas* of maize for every *almud* planted on approximately one hectare of land. After the landlord takes away his 2 *fanegas*, there are still 6 *fanegas* per hectare left for the Zinacanteco farmer. An average family consumes about 5 *fanegas* of maize a year. Thus, average to good years leave surpluses for the Zinacantecos to sell in the markets, which help pay for their expensive rituals. Only in rare bad years will he lose on his investment of seed and labor.

There is still a major operation to be performed, for the piles of shelled maize are six hours or more walking distance (or two- to three-hours trucking distance) from home. Some maize is still carried on Zinacanteco backs with tumplines, but more is now carried by horses or mules or, in recent years, by trucks which haul the maize to a point near the Zinacantecos' Highland homes.

Once the maize is home, each man takes his share to his granary, which may be a separate structure or a bin in the corner of his house. In either case, it is always "protected" by placing a small wooden cross into the middle of the pile of stored corn. The cross is decorated with flowers and surrounded by several unhusked ears of corn, defined as "mother" and "father" of the maize. The family now uses some of the maize for food—which brings the women into the maize cycle for the first time—and the men sell the surplus in the market.

The most important maize food consumed by Zinacantecos is tortillas. An adult male ordinarily eats about six to ten tortillas at each of his three daily meals when he is at home. But while the man's part in the maize cycle is largely finished (except for eating), the woman's work has just begun.

There are three basic processes in the production of tortillas: boiling the maize kernels in lime water to soften them; grinding the kernels on a metate or in a corn mill to make the dough; and patting out and cooking the tortillas.

The women bring the maize from the granary in baskets, and pour it into

Photo 9. Zinacanteco woman patting out tortillas and cooking them on a comal *(left) placed over the three hearthstones inside the house.* (Photo by Frank Cancian)

cooking pots to which they add water and lime. (The men make lime by heating limestone with a hot fire; the powdered lime is then slaked by mixing it with water and made into lumps and dried in the sun.) The pots are placed on the fire to boil until the kernels become soft, and then lifted off and placed in the corner to cool.

After being washed, the kernels were traditionally placed on a metate to be ground, ordinarily two or three times. The metates in use in Zinacantan are three-legged types made of basalt in the neighboring Chamulas and sold in the market in Chamula or in San Cristobal. They are placed on a board that raises them about 12 inches off the floor and makes it easier for women to grind in a kneeling position. Today the kernels are much more commonly carried in a bucket to the closest corn-grinding mill (powered either by electricity or by a gasoline engine) for the first grinding. The flour is then brought back home to be given another grinding on metates, or, in some cases, run through a hand-turned grinder until it is fine enough for tortillas.

The traditional grinding process was long and arduous. Women would start in the morning between 5 and 6 and it was often 8 a.m. before they had produced enough tortillas for the day's meals. Now the process has been speeded up when mechanical mills do the first grinding.

As soon as a woman has enough dough ground, she begins to pat out tortillas and to cook them. The creation of the tortillas is done in various ways: some households still use the back-and-forth patting motion; others pat out the tortillas on a piece of wax paper on a small round stool; and still others possess ingenious tortilla presses with handles, purchased in San Cristobal. The cooking is done on a slightly concave, round clay or metal *comal*, about 2 feet in diameter, that is propped up over the fire on three hearth stones. The tortillas are cooked about thirty seconds on each side and then placed in a dry gourd container to keep them warm until served or to store for eating later in the day.

Once the cooking begins, a remarkably efficient set of operations is in process. A woman may simultaneously be grinding additional corn, stopping to pat out tortillas when more are needed, and cooking tortillas on the *comal*. All the materials and instruments are within her reach from her kneeling position at the metate. She can shift easily from one activity to another in this tortilla-making position, while her husband and sons sit on small chairs by the fire, warming themselves, and waiting hungrily, until she has produced enough to feed them their morning meal.

A longer process is necessary to produce the large toasted tortillas, which last for several days (ordinary tortillas mildew within forty-eight hours) and can be carried by the men in large baskets or cloth sacks to the Lowlands to feed themselves while they are away farming. The toasted tortillas must be propped up around the fire and heated for at least ten or fifteen minutes.

Two other types of maize foods made from the ground dough are important. *Pozol* is a ball of dough taken by men to the fields. It sours after a day or two, but until then can be used to provide nourishment. A small piece of the dough is broken off and added to water in a bowl or open gourd, and the mixture is drunk.

Atole is a highly prized corn gruel made by boiling the corn dough in water and adding brown sugar. It is heavy and sweet, but tasty and highly nourishing. *Atole* is always served by Zinacanteco families on festive occasions.

BEANS

Next to maize, the most important domesticated food plants grown by the Zinacantecos are beans, a crucial source of protein in a diet that is very short on meat. In the Highlands, several varieties of beans are planted in the same holes with the maize and grow at the base of the maize stalks. More important are the beans planted between the rows of maize when the stalks are bent over in the Lowland fields. In good years an *almud* of seed planted will yield a *fanega* of beans. The bean pods are pulled off the plants by hand and threshed either by hand or by pounding with a stick. Surpluses are sold in the market; the rest are kept stored in large jars or sacks for eating by the family during the year. Beans are eaten mainly boiled, but are also used for special dishes, such as the bean tamales that are served at weddings.

SQUASHES

The third most important crop is squash. Some varieties are planted in the same holes with the maize, but more are planted at the edges of the cornfields. Two closely related gourd plants are cultivated for containers: the *tecomates*, with the shape of a figure eight, which are used for carrying water while traveling or working in the fields and (in small form) for whistles in curing ceremonies to summon the lost parts of the "inner soul"; and the *toles*, which serve as plates and bowls for serving and storing food, especially tortillas.

HUNTING AND GATHERING

Hunting animals for food is no longer of great importance to the Zinacanteco diet. An occasional rabbit is shot, and hunters from the parajes close to the Lowlands bag deer from time to time. But the Chiapas Highlands have been populated so densely for such a long period of time that almost all forms of edible mammals have been long since hunted off.

On the other hand, there is relatively full exploitation of edible wild plants, insects, snails, and iguanas. Various types of wild greens are gathered and cooked, and at least sixteen different varieties of mushrooms are recognized and collected for food. Two types of snails are collected, and iguanas are considered such a delicacy that they are sometimes substituted for chicken in ritual meals. Finally, like their Maya ancestors, the Zinacantecos are extraordinarily fond of honey, which they collect from wild beehives in the woods.

DOMESTICATED ANIMALS

If the ancestors of the Zinacantecos had domesticated animals in pre-Columbian times, they must have had only dogs and turkeys. Most houses now have one or more dogs, and there are a few turkeys. But much more important now are the domesticated animals that came with the Spanish: chickens, sheep, horses, and mules.

Almost all Zinacanteco households maintain a flock of ten to fifteen chickens, which are owned and tended by the women. The chickens are red, white, and black, but black is the favorite color, since only black chickens can serve for sacrifices in curing ceremonies. Some families have chicken coops, but most of the chickens merely roost in trees at the edge of the house. The chickens are killed and eaten mainly for ritual meals. The eggs are sometimes eaten, but are more frequently sold to add to the family's cash income.

Horses and mules are owned by the men, but are almost never ridden by Zinacantecos, except during the ritual "horse races" during the Fiestas of San Lorenzo and San Sebastián in the Ceremonial Center. Rather, they are reserved for carrying heavy loads: toasted tortillas from homes to lowland fields, maize from lowland fields to homes or to market. (The men never own or use burros, because these animals cannot keep up with fast-traveling Zinacantecos.) The horses and mules are never pastured, but are always staked out for grazing. This means that a man must constantly watch his animals, take them to water, and change their tethering territory periodically.

Zinacanteco sheep are owned and tended entirely by the women. They are never butchered for mutton, but are kept for their wool, which the women weave into clothing on back-strap looms. The sheep are kept at night in small rectangular corrals constructed of vertical planks, which can be taken apart and transported to different locations to fertilize the small field plots around the house (see above). During the day the herds (never more than about thirty animals) are let out to graze and taken to water and herded by one of the women or a couple of the small daughters.

CLOTHING

The sheep are sheared three times a year with scissors purchased in San Cristobal. The fleece is washed with a wild root. The white wool is either left its natural shade for white yarn, or dyed black, using native dye, or red or green, using store-bought dyes. The wool is carded, spun, and then woven into warm *chamarras* and blankets for the men, and into shawls for the women.

The women also weave cotton thread, purchased in San Cristobal, into short pants, shirts, and light-weight chamarras for the men, and skirts for the women. The checkered kerchiefs worn around the necks of the men, and the blouses of the women are the only items for which the cloth is purchased. The men weave their own hats from strips of palm, and purchase sandals made either by Ladinos in San Cristobal or by the Chamulas. The women go bare-footed.

In recent years most of the men have started wearing long trousers purchased from Ladinos in the San Cristobal market, and the traditional short pants are worn mainly for ceremonial occasions. There is now also less weaving of hats because, increasingly, the men either go bare-headed or wear hats purchased in San Cristobal. However, the traditional hats of palm strips are still worn in ritual settings.

These clothing styles are perhaps the most striking feature of Zinacanteco culture and they have high symbolic value. Their styles readily indicate who is a Zinacanteco, as opposed to some other type of Indian in Chiapas, since all men and all women in a municipio dress alike. There is strong emphasis upon having new and clean clothing, not only for important fiestas (when the women are frantically busy weaving for weeks in advance) but also for curing ceremonies. A special clothes-washer is always appointed to wash a patient's clothes in a particular waterhole, and these clothes are also later incensed over copal incense before they are placed on the patient. Further, there is a strong belief that the Ancestral Gods will punish a person who goes about in dirty clothes.

Photo 10. A young Zinacanteco boy in typical dress. (Photo by Frank Cancian)

Sacred objects, as well as people, have clothing in Zinacantan, and the emphasis upon new and clean clothes is applied equally to them. The saint images in the temples are clothed elaborately, and their clothes must be washed and incensed periodically, with new clothing provided when the others become too old. The crosses at mountain, waterhole, and cave shrines are "clothed" in fresh pinetree tops and flowers, and these must be renewed for each ceremonial occasion.

The clothing styles are reminiscent of those that we infer for the ancient Maya, who are shown in painted wall murals and on stelae wearing elaborate head-gear, capes, sandals, and jewelry of various types. It is obvious that contemporary Zinacanteco costumes are derived in part from aboriginal elements and in part from Spanish colonial styles. It seems quite likely that some elements, such as the high-backed sandals worn by Zinacantecos on ritual occasions, are direct survivals from Maya Classic times. They closely resemble the sandals on men pictured at such archaeological sites as Palenque and Bonampak. Other elements appear to be functional substitutions for aboriginal styles, such as the multicolored ribbon streamers on the men's hats, which are probably the contemporary version of the feathered head-dresses worn by the ancient Maya men.

MARKETS

Although Zinacantecos are participating in a subsistence economy—growing and collecting most of their own food, making their own houses, and weaving much of their own clothing—they have been involved in marketing and trade with other Indians for centuries and with Ladinos since the Spanish Conquest. They are also increasingly involved in wage-labor jobs in San Cristobal, Tuxtla Gutierrez, and elsewhere in southern Mexico.

There is good historical evidence that the Zinacantecos traded goods with Aztec merchants from central Mexico in prehispanic times. They have certainly been salt merchants since early Colonial times, and perhaps before, and they have a well-deserved reputation for being very astute in matters of trade and marketing. Little of the traveling they do now to San Cristobal, to Tuxtla Gutierrez, and to other Indian towns is motivated by desires to visit or to "see the sights." Rather they are going to market. Similarly, when there is a large fiesta in Zinacantan Center, the market is always one of the major reasons why Zinacantecos come to the fiesta and the trade is brisk.

The most important products the Zinacanteco men have to offer for sale are surplus maize, secondarily beans and, increasingly, flowers grown for the Ladino markets in both San Cristobal and Tuxtla Gutierrez, as well as other cities in Mexico. The women are now also weaving and selling items of clothing for the tourist trade in San Cristobal. A large number of Zinacantecos specialize in the salt trade. They purchase the salt at the salt works near Ixtapa in long cylindrical cakes, and carry them on horse or mule back or by truck to fiesta day markets in Zinacantan, to regular Sunday markets in Indian towns such as Chamula and San Andres Larrainzar, or to the daily market in San Cristobal. Here the salt is sold in blocks sawed from the cylindrical cakes. Minor items sold by Zinacantecos include eggs and fruit, especially peaches; a few women sell tortillas, both plain and toasted, while a few men sell reeds for the sticks used to construct sky rockets.

The major items purchased by the Zinacantecos in markets or stores in San Cristobal, or in other Indian towns, can be summarized as follows. For their ceremonials, they purchase rum liquor, candles, sky rockets, incense, cigarettes, and musical instruments. For their houses, they buy kerosene and small kerosene lamps, as well as light bulbs as more and more hamlets are reached by electricity. They also purchase locks, flashlights, metates, comals, cooking pots (made in Chamula), water jugs (made in Aguacatenango), and furniture—mainly small tables and chairs (also made in Chamula). For their fields and for wood-gathering, they purchase axes, machetes, hoes, and bill hooks, as well as commercial fertilizers and chemical weed-killers and the sprayers to spread the chemical solution on the weeds. For food, they buy coffee, beer, soda pop, wheat flour rolls, brown sugar, fish products, pork, beef, and fruits—especially mangos, bananas, pineapples, and melons. For clothing, they purchase cotton thread and cotton cloth, palm for men's hats, sandals, net and leather shoulder bags, rubberized ponchos or plastic raincoats and plastic boots for rainy days, kerchiefs, colored ribbons, and the large black hats worn by upper-level cargoholders. Finally, the Zinacantecos are purchasing trucks, VW microbusses, busses, and passenger cars in increasing numbers.

Special mention should be made of the importance of the *posh*, the rum liquor called *aguardiente* in Spanish, which is produced either legally by La-dinos in their commercial distilleries, or illegally by the neighboring Chamulas in their home-made stills. The bootleg Chamula liquor is cheaper and usually of better quality, and hence Zinacantecos prefer it for their ceremonies, especially since this liquor is the most expensive purchase that must be made for every ritual occasion.

The marketing patterns that have evolved over time for Zinacantecos involve them in various transactions outside their tribal boundaries and have a number of critical economic functions.

The transactions that occur are a means of exchanging goods between (a) the Highlands and the Lowlands, (b) the Indians and the Ladinos in this bi-cultural society; (c) the outside industrial world and the local peasant world, and (d) the various Indian towns that specialize in different products.

The Highland-Lowland exchange in Chiapas represents in microcosm the kind of economic transaction crucial in many parts of Middle America in making for a "richer" economic life. An ordinary meal for a Zinacanteco man at home consists of tortillas and a bowl of beans seasoned with salt. But this monotonous diet may be varied by the addition of other cultivated plants, like chile or squash, or by wild plants or mushrooms. Ritual meals provide an even more important addition to the diet, because either chicken, pork, or fish (and, on some large ceremonial occasions, beef) must be served along with liquor, coffee, and rolls. But the seasons and the participation of the Zinacantecos in both a Highland and Lowland environment account for even more variety. In the late Spring the Zinacantecos consume enormous quantities of mangos brought up from the Lowlands; summer brings fresh green corn, ripening squashes and a variety of fruits such as Highland peaches and apples and Lowland pineapples and melons. But even the basic subsistence crops of maize and beans are harvested at different seasons at varying altitudes, and hence the Highland-Lowland exchange keeps more of these foodstuffs available.

The Indian-Ladino exchange is also fundamental to the economic system, with the Indians generally providing the basic foodstuffs and labor for the Ladinos, and the latter providing mainly ritual and decorative products for the Indians. The Zinacantecos bring in corn, beans, and salt for the Ladinos, and the Ladinos provide the Zinacantecos with liquor, ribbons, candles, sky rockets, beef, pork, and Catholic priests—all for ritual.

The exchange between the outside industrial world and local peasant world is, of course, also involved in the Indian-Ladino transactions, in that the hardware stores where the Indians purchase their hoes, machetes, flashlights, electric light bulbs, and metal locks are also owned by Ladino merchants.

Finally, the economic transactions continue a pattern of trade between Indian municipios, each specializing in the production of different goods, that was undoubtedly active in aboriginal times. While Zinacantan produces surplus corn and salt, Amatenango produces water jugs, Tenejapa produces peanuts, and Chamula produces a variety of other goods, ranging from guitars to metates and liquor.

WAGE WORK

In the last twenty-five years many Zinacantecos have left agriculture and become dependent upon wage work. Our field studies in the 1960s showed that almost every man grew enough maize for his family's needs, as well as sufficient surplus to sell in the market in order to purchase other commodities. Some younger men worked in road construction, especially on the Pan American Highway, but turned to farming maize as soon as they could. Older men took occasional wage labor jobs and/or supplemented their income by trading activities (Cancian 1987).

When the economy was studied again in detail in the 1980s we discovered that the situation had undergone marked changes. For example, in 1967 the hamlet of *Na Chih* had only nine men who depended upon sources of income other than maize farming; by 1983 the same hamlet had 130 men (40 percent of the married heads of households) with no maize fields at all and who were entirely dependent upon other forms of economic activity (Cancian 1987). In 1981 in the hamlet of *'Apas* nearly 75 percent of the married heads of households engaged partially or exclusively in wage work (Collier 1989).

The shift in economic activity took place both because less land was available to the ever-growing Zinacanteco population and because alternative opportunities became attractive. The decline in land available for rental by the Zinacantecos in the Grijalva Lowlands was due to increased cattle production on the part of the Ladino landlords and to the flooding of huge areas (formerly farmed by the Zinacantecos) after the completion of hydroelectric dams (Cancian 1987).

On the other hand, the hydroelectric projects and Mexico's temporary oil boom of the late 1970s and early 1980s created increased demand for construction labor in the 1970s, both in Chiapas and in the neighboring state of Tabasco. As a consequence, many more Zinacanteco men became wage workers. Since the end of the oil boom in 1982, most of these wage workers have returned to Zinacantan, where some have opted for maize farming utilizing chemical fertilizers and weed-killers on less productive land. Others have devoted their efforts to cultivating flowers and fruit trees; still others have found various jobs with the Mexican government programs or in Ladino enterprises in towns in the Highlands of Chiapas.

BORROWING MONEY

Since Zinacantecos participate in a money economy, we might ask how they acquire enough Mexican pesos to purchase market products for daily use and for their expensive rituals. A few Zinacantecos save money and store it away for future use, but most of them rely rather on a complicated set of loaning and borrowing customs. When a Zinacanteco needs money, he goes to another Zinacanteco, most frequently a *compadre* (See Chapter 6), bearing a bottle of rum liquor. He goes through the proper greetings as he arrives at the house of the potential lender, then presents the bottle. If the potential lender accepts the bottle, he is obligated to give the loan. There is, therefore, patterned hesitancy (if not outright refusal) to accept the bottle unless the motives of the visitor can be ascertained. If the bottle is accepted, ritual drinking begins and the visitor completes his request for the loan, stating in detail why he needs the money. The loan is then given, or promised for a future specified date, and more drinking takes place. There are some recognized variations in the pattern. For example, a potential borrower may arrive with two bottles and ask for 20,000 pesos. The lender may choose to accept only one bottle and loan only 10,000 pesos.

In the case of loans to pay for curing ceremonies or for the expenses of a cargo, it is not considered polite to ask for the return of the loan until the lender has some emergency need for the cash. For example, if a time is approaching when the lender is going to be installed in a cargo position, it is quite proper to go to the borrower and ask for the return of the pesos.

The test case of this procedure occurred during 1959–1960, when one of our fieldworkers had loaned out some 5,000 pesos to various Zinacantecos. He discovered that near the end of his field trip he could quite acceptably approach his debtors and say, "I am about to leave for Boston by plane. The cost of the ticket is almost 4000 pesos for myself and wife and baby and now I need the money." He managed to collect all but 500 pesos.

Loans for purposes other than curing ceremonies or cargos are more likely to be due on a fixed date, and the lender ordinarily asks for interest. The rates of interest are high by our standards, varying between 10 and 20 percent per month.

BECOMING ENTREPRENEURS

Beyond borrowing money, an even more lucrative possibility has emerged for accumulating enough Mexican pesos to serve in prestigious positions in the cargo system and to pay for domestic rituals, such as curing ceremonies: to become a large, entrepreneur-type maize-farmer on lands rented from Ladinos in the Lowlands. Really successful operators are able to borrow money from Mexican government banks, hire laborers (mainly Chamulas), and plant up to 15 hectares of land in maize. In good years the surpluses are such that these farmers can not only supply family food with ease, but can hold the surpluses for the best possible profits in the market in late summer.

More recently, many of the wealthy Zinacantecos have shifted to commerce, especially as truckers and vendors transporting and selling agricultural crops throughout the state of Chiapas (Collier 1989). These truck owners (whom Frank Cancian describes as the emerging economic elite) have managed to borrow enough from banks and individuals to purchase and maintain fleets of vehicles that provide transportation for Zinacanteco passengers and goods to and from markets.

The surplus cash controlled by these large operators is impressive by Zinacanteco standards, and it can be converted into much more rapid movement through the cargo system and an achievement of power and prestige that reaches well beyond the potential for men without land or trucks and entrepreneurial skill.

To date, most of this surplus continues to be poured into the ritual system. To be sure, new houses may be built of adobe brick and tile roofs to replace the smaller thatched structures, a man might own two flashlights rather than one, and the family may eat chicken and beef more often. But these expenditures are minor compared to the cost of an expensive cargo position in the Ceremonial Center.

Hence, while surpluses are being made by a segment of Zinacantecos, expenditures serve mainly to shift the resources from the private to the public sector in the costs of ceremonial life. The system has not reached the point in which surpluses go into capital resources, except in the case of purchases of trucks and buses. Beyond this, the economic system is likely to continue at its present level of balance among subsistence farming, trading salt, growing and marketing flowers and fruit and other crops, and wage work for at least another generation or two.

6/The Life Cycle

The life cycle for individual Zinacantecos begins when a midwife performs at a new birth and ends when the person dies and is buried with much ceremony in one of the cemeteries. In between, the notable points in the cycle may be summarized by describing the baptism and socialization of children, the intricate patterns of courtship and marriage, and the strategies that Zinacantecos follow in working their way through the cargo system.

BIRTH

Zinacanteco births take place at home with the aid of a midwife who is selected in the sixth or seventh month of pregnancy. The midwife visits the pregnant mother every week, and lightly massages the woman's stomach. When labor begins, the midwife is summoned. The woman kneels on a reed mat on the earthen floor while her husband stands behind her, pulling her sash tight, and one of the other male relatives sits on a chair facing her, seizing her by the shoulders to support her during each labor pain. All of the participants (except for the mother) are served rum during both the period of labor and the birth (Anschuetz 1966).

As soon as the baby is born, the midwife takes over. The umbilical cord is tied a handspan from the infant, and then cut with the point of a heated machete. The cord and the afterbirth are wrapped in rags and buried in the patio. Then the midwife cleans the new baby with a dry rag.

Within an hour after birth a ritual is performed to symbolize the sex-identity of the new baby. The midwife holds the infant, and objects that will be used in the child's later life are placed in both of its fists. If the infant is a boy, he is presented with a digging stick, a hoe, and a billhook (which he will use to farm maize when he grows up), as well as an axe and a splinter of pitch pine (so that he will know how to go out with a torch to meet his father coming home in the dark). A girl is presented with a *mano* (which she will use to grind maize), and various parts of a back-strap loom (which she will one day use in weaving). The baby is then given to the mother, and both are wrapped up in blankets and virtually hidden from view.

The day after the birth, the midwife comes to take the first of three sweat baths with the mother. They enter the sweathouse together, and the midwife washes the mother with myrtle and laurel leaves. The mother is then placed back in bed, and the midwife is offered a ritual meal, during the course of which five bottles of liquor are served and all of the women present bow to the midwife, thanking her for her services.

The second day after the birth, the baby is formally presented to everyone in the house, who embrace it, kiss it, and blow in each of its ears. For four or five days no one talks much to the mother, and visitors are not welcome.

The mother must take two more sweat baths with the midwife, who returns every two days after the birth for this purpose and is given a ritual meal each time.

The mother continues to be treated delicately for about three weeks, during which time she must observe certain food restrictions. She does not wander out of the house, except to relieve herself or to take sweat baths with the midwife. Nor does she do any work. Even when the mother starts working again, she continues to keep the baby wrapped up and hidden from view. All of this shielding of the infant is believed to be necessary to keep the "inner soul" in its body.

During the first three or four months, the infant continues to interact almost exclusively with its mother and to receive almost constant care, love, and affection. The baby is seldom separated from the mother (or some other female in the household) for more than a few minutes. It is either nursing (whenever it cries), wrapped in a shawl and carried on the mother's back, or asleep beside the mother in bed. There continues to be great concern for the infant's "inner soul" during this period, for it is believed that the soul is very loosely attached to the infant's body. Extreme care is exercised until the infant is baptized, a rite ordinarily performed during the first three or four months, and usually within a month after the baby's birth.

An interesting discovery about Zinacanteco infants made by pediatricians and developmental psychologists working with us in the field is how relatively quiet they are compared to babies in our society. To quote from a recent article:

> Zinacanteco infants, quiet and alert, attentively observed their surroundings, lay-ing the foundation for later observational learning. They did not cry intensely or flail about, demanding that someone react to them (Greenfield, Brazelton, and Childs 1989).

The interpretation of this difference is that it is partly genetic and partly cultural. The low level of physical activity, present at birth, is reinforced by the swaddling and by keeping the infant in the mother's shawl, either on the mother's back or nursing at the mother's breasts. Such behavior is adaptive to the Zinacanteco style of life, in which the whole family lives in one room with an open fire. A hyperactive American infant would not only be disruptive to this type of family life but would be likely to burn himself in the open fire or cut himself with a sharp machete.

BAPTISM

The baptismal rite is extremely important to the Zinacantecos—in fact, the most important of the seven Catholic sacraments—not only to "fix" the infant's "inner soul" in its body, but also to create bonds of ritual kinship, called *compadrazgo*, for the parents.

In the Catholic and Episcopal Churches of the United States, "godfathers" and "godmothers" are selected to participate in the baptism (or christening) of a child. Following the sacramental rite, a reciprocal relationship is established between the "godparents" and "godchild." These terms are often used to refer to the persons involved, but never as terms of address. Following Church doctrine, it is the duty of the "godparents" to ensure that the "godchild" has proper religious instruction and is duly confirmed at the appropriate time. Although the parents of the child and the "godparents" are normally either relatives or close friends, they do not address or refer to one another by special terms, nor do they have any very special mutual relationship. The relationship that continues to be important, if any relationship persists at all, is between "godparents" and the "godchild."

In Southern Europe, and in the Latin American cultures derived from them, this system of ritual kinship takes on important new dimensions. The crucial bond established is not between the godparents and godchild, but rather between the godparents and parents of the child. The adults involved in the system all address and refer to each other (in Spanish) as *compadre* or *comadre*, depending upon the sex of the person being addressed. Furthermore, the bond established normally involves mutual rights and obligations, such as economic, political, or social assistance. The relationship between godparents and godchild is either de-emphasized or highly perfunctory, and often ignored except as a reference point for establishing the all-important *compadrazgo* bonds.

The Zinacantecos obviously acquired this ritual kinship system from the Spanish during the Colonial Period, but they have carried the system much further in the sense that compadres can be acquired in a variety of ways, and in large numbers. Not only are ritual kinsmen acquired with the sacramental rites of baptism, confirmation, and marriage performed by the priest in a Catholic church, but literally dozens of compadres are added, by extension, in the ritual meals at home following the rites of baptism and confirmation, and more especially in the "house entering" and "wedding ceremonies" (see below).

Compadres for baptism are selected by Zinacantecos with four considerations in mind. First, they must be members of another patrilineage, meaning they must have a different Indian surname. Second, the same godparents should also be called upon to serve for three children of a family. Third, the godparents should live nearby. Finally, they should be willing and able to provide economic and political services in the future, which means the godfather has passed a cargo, is a respected member of the community, and is relatively well-to-do.

The baptismal rite may be performed either in the church of San Lorenzo in Zinacantan or at the cathedral in San Cristobal where a priest is always on duty. On the appointed day, the father picks up the godparents and the two couples go to the church with the infant. Two white candles are purchased, one to be held by each godparent. At the church, the candles are lighted, and the infant is transferred to the godparent of the same sex while each godparent holds a candle. The priest then recites a prayer, places a piece of salt in the infant's mouth, makes the sign of the cross over the forehead, mouth, and chest, and touches his stole to the infant's head and then bathes it in Holy Water. The infant has now been through all the necessary Catholic ritual, but the Zinacanteco ritual continues. The godparents return home with the parents and are served a formal ritual meal, normally attended by the grandparents and other close relatives, and sometimes friendly neighbors as well. In the Zinacanteco view, these persons all become ritual kinsmen of the new godparents.

The moment the new social link is established, the persons who address each other as *kumpare* and *kumale* (in Tzotzil) acquire special lifetime rights and obligations toward one another. For a man, a compadre can be called upon to loan money, help build a house, become an assistant in a ceremony, or assist in political crises. For a woman, a comadre may be called upon to loan money, help make tortillas on ritual occasions, or serve as a confidante in an exchange of gossip. For both men and women, the relationship is important for hospitality that is offered when one is traveling. In a word, the compadrazgo network provides a pool of people to whom one can turn for money, labor, credit, political support, and hospitality.

SOCIALIZATION

After about four months, the infant's interaction expands to include the other household members, all of whom cuddle and play with the baby (Edwards 1989). By the age of one to one-and-a-half, the infant crawls and/or walks about freely, and the nurturant treatment begins to change. He no longer spends most of the day tied by a shawl to the back of his mother or older sister, but is increasingly allowed to walk on his own. However, he is still carefully watched so that he will not fall ill and lose his "inner soul," even though he is expected to know enough to stay out of the fire and walk among the axes and machetes without hurting himself. Severe scoldings, or other forms of punishment, are extremely rare. Only if a child bites his mother's nipple while nursing will he be struck.

By the time an infant is walking competently, expectations increase, and he is scolded for failure to comply. He is expected to keep clear of the hearth and out of puddles, and to notify an older member of the family when he has to urinate or defecate. He is also expected not to bother the mother when she is very busy grinding maize or weaving. There is little pressure to master the basic skills of walking, talking, and learning to urinate or defecate outside, and little or no pride on the part of parents over the speed with which children learn these skills. Rather, the interaction consists of repetition of words and phrases in a playful, affectionate tone that helps the infant learn.

The nurturant phase ends when a new baby is born to the mother. The older child is then usually completely weaned. At first, the adults make an effort to give the displaced child extra attention and cater to his tantrums. But for a boy or girl between about three and nine, life becomes rough. Other members of the family give little affection, but instead command him to perform errands, generally maintaining an attitude of "don't bother me." The situation is especially difficult for a boy whose father may be away farming maize in the Lowlands. If he is too young to go along, he must spend his time in a predominantly female environment, with the young sisters paying more attention to each other and to the new baby, and the older sisters and mother busily running the household. He may be called upon to perform small tasks, such as bringing in the chickens or playing with the baby, but most of the time he is expected to amuse himself.

While the girls are busy performing chores leading directly to the skills needed for an adult woman's role (weaving, cooking, tending children, and fetching water and wood), a boy's chores are primarily feminine work and do not prepare him adequately for the heavy farming work he will later be required to do.

While between the ages of about three and nine, boys and girls often play together in groups, but the period between nine and adulthood is characterized by a rigid separation of the sexes. By the time they are nine or ten, boys begin to go with their fathers to the Lowlands. By the age of twelve to fourteen, boys are believed to be "formed." They may travel to and from the Lowlands alone, and are able to take down loads of toasted tortillas for the farming groups and return with loads of maize. When they are at home, they often wander around together with groups of related boys, watching for the approach of strangers and going out in groups to visit with them. They sometimes go to San Cristobal together to buy and sell in the market. But their "adolescence" does not last long. By the age of sixteen or seventeen, the boys begin to think about becoming engaged, and start to work hard to accumulate their share of the money needed for the long courtship (see below).

By the age of seven or eight, most girls begin to make a substantial contribution to the work of the household, and by ten or eleven almost all of them are constantly busy helping the adult women grind maize, make tortillas, fetch water and wood, herd sheep, tend younger children, sweep out the house, and so on. They also begin to learn to weave (by observing their mothers at their looms), since one of the essential qualities for a Zinacanteco woman is to be able to weave good clothes for herself and her future husband. By the age of fifteen or sixteen, the girl is usually engaged, and by seventeen or eighteen, she is normally married.

During the age of socialization, there is little formal instruction in Zinacantan about the sacred values of the culture or about the ritual procedure

Photo 11. Zinacanteco parents are very affectionate with their children. (Photo by Frank Cancian)

and prayers learned and performed by any competent adult. Sacred stories about the gods and their activities are sometimes told around the hearth at night by the father; and these stories are frequently related during the lonely nights in the Lowlands while the men are away from home. Experiences involving beliefs about the "souls" are often shared in conversation. But even more learning takes place by virtue of the fact that people live in one-roomed houses, and hence when a shaman comes to diagnose an illness, or returns later to perform a curing ceremony, small children observe the proceedings as a matter of course. When the children are very small, they sleep through the all-night ceremonies. But as they become older, they stay awake longer and longer, and are called upon to help with the ceremonies. The boys are pressed into duty as assistants for the shamans. The girls help their mothers to prepare the ritual meals. In addition, children are taken to ceremonies in Zinacantan Center beginning at an early age. By the time Zinacantecos become adults they have learned an immense range of ritual procedures and prayers for ceremonies.

An increasing proportion of Zinacanteco children attend the formal schools of the Mexican government, where they are taught the elements of reading, writing, and arithmetic, and something of the history of Mexico. They ordinarily stay in school only about three or four years, with the result that most young Zinacantecos are able to read and write, at least haltingly, in Spanish.

The major problems in Zinacanteco socialization appear to occur between the ages of three, after weaning has occurred, and nine, when the boys begin to accompany their fathers to the Lowlands and the girls begin to be of genuine utility in the household. A drastic shift occurs from a period of being cared for and shown affection to one of being relatively neglected and ordered about. There is evidence of fairly intense sibling rivalry among brothers, which in part may have to do with competition for inherited land, but is exacerbated by the treatment given boys between ages three and nine. For girls, the situation is different. Sisters are separated at the adult stage by patrilocal residence at marriage, and there is little evidence of tension between them. While a younger brother spends his life in a struggle for status in a system that has led his older brother to resent him, a girl's situation is quite different— she moves after marriage and has the problem of getting along with the husband's parents.

COURTSHIP AND MARRIAGE

When a Zinacanteco boy reaches the age of sixteen or seventeen, he begins to think of marriage and to look over the available girls among those he sees along the paths, at fiestas, or visiting in the homes of relatives (see Jane Collier 1968). The courtship and marriage that follow the boy's selection involve complicated social and economic transactions and complex rituals that focus upon taking the wife away from her domestic group and installing her permanently in her husband's group. There are also important by-products, such as the establishment of many new compadrazgo and affinal kin ties, and the definition of the new couple as full adult members of the community. Among other things, a young man cannot properly serve in an important cargo position until he is married.

The first step in courtship is for the boy to persuade his parents he has made a wise choice and enlist their aid in the expenses that will follow. The boy and the parents then select two "petitioners," respected men who have the reputation for being good speakers, and enlist their services by calling upon them with bottles of liquor. Meanwhile, the boy busies himself learning all that he can about the daily habits and future plans of his chosen bride's father, information he will use to plan his strategy for the formal petition.

On the appointed day of the petition, the two petitioners and their wives come to the boy's house when they are told, for the first time, the name of the girl who has been selected. Secrecy is necessary so that the father of the girl will not hear of the impending petition and leave home to avoid giving away his daughter.

The boy's family, accompanied by the petitioners, walk to the girl's house; the boy's mother carries a basket of gifts, including chocolate, brown sugar, and rolls, and the boy carries a 20-liter jug of rum. Arriving at the girl's house well after dark, they wait quietly outside while assistants surround the house. One of the petitioners then calls to the people inside, asking to borrow a flashlight or an axe, or making some other request that will get the door open. Then the petitioners and their wives rush inside, while the girl's family attempts to escape through the back door, only to be stopped by the helpers. The petitioners then kneel in front of the girl's father, place bottles of liquor at his feet, and begin their request, while the women in the boy's group plead with the girl's mother. Since the phrases are traditional, both sides talk at once, without listening carefully to each other. The only person who is silent is the girl, who sits apart with her eyes downcast and her shawl drawn over her mouth.

A typical dialogue follows:

> *The petitioners*: "May your head speak, may your heart speak. Seize my words, beloved father (or mother). Today I speak because of your mud, your earth (metaphorical way of referring to the girl). Don't cut out my child's heart.

> *The father (or mother) of the girl*: "Your child is a devil, he drinks too much. I won't give my child. I won't give her to suffering, to beating, to scolding. With difficulty I raised her, talked to her. Get out! Leave! If I want, I'll look for you with words. Get out! Leave! Take your water (liquor)!

The pleading continues through the long night, as the drink-pourer tries to serve liquor to the father of the girl and the petitioners take turns on their knees on the hard earthen floor. The father of the girl steadfastly refuses the liquor.

Finally, if the father gives in and accepts his first shot of liquor, then the long courtship formally begins. The petitioners move from their kneeling position to chairs, and the boy is brought in to meet his future father-in-law. The boy kneels, asks pardon for having come into the house, and promises in a long speech to be a good son-in-law. He then serves the girl's father and all her relatives a shot of liquor, and the drinking continues until the jug is empty and everyone is drunk. The petitioners then depart, leaving the boy to help his future parents-in-law to bed, and to greet their hangovers in the morning with additional liquor. When they are on their feet and relatively sober, he may return home. From this point on, the boy begins to use kin terms to address his future wife's family, but he is the only one to enter into the web of kinship at this time. The early phases of courtship are a trial period, and if it doesn't work, the only kin tie that must be severed is that between the boy and his fiancee's family.

A year or more then elapses before the next major ceremony—"entering the house"—and during this period the ties between the two families are gradually cemented by the boy's payment of a bride price. As a Zinacanteco informant expressed it, "little by little the boy pays, little by little he removes the girl."

The payments take three forms: large nets of fruit and rum liquor at the time of major fiestas when choice Lowland fruits can be purchased in the fiesta markets; smaller gifts of maize, beans, tortillas, and liquor every two or three weeks; and work that the boy does for the father-in-law in the fields or around the house.

Within two years, the girl's father, who has kept a careful account of the boy's expenditures and labor, may decide the boy has invested enough in the girl and suggest that the "house entering" ceremony take place. However, if the girl's family does not take the initiative, the boy's family does so as soon as it decides enough has been spent for the bride price.

Once the date has been set, the girl's family appoints an old woman to accompany the girl and a ritual advisor (*totilme'il*, an old, ritually-experienced man) to serve as master of ceremonies. The boy's family, with the petitioners, arrives bearing a burlap bag containing a gift of maize, beans, meat, and a blanket, as well as rolls, coffee, and liquor to serve the girl's family. This time all are welcomed into the house by the "master of ceremonies," except for the boy who waits outside with his gift of maize, beans, and meat, and his blanket. After two rounds of rolls, coffee, and liquor, the petitioners ask the girl's father to allow the boy to enter. The boy is brought in and seated with the girl's relatives.

After the third round of rolls, coffee, and liquor, the girl's father is asked to name the "embracer" of the wedding. Then the girl is led over to the boy's side where she bows to her future parents-in-law and begins to address them and the other relatives of the boy by kin terms. The petitioners go to ask the embracer to serve, placing gifts at his feet and saying: "Will you take the 'inner souls' of our children under your care?" Once the embracer accepts, he (and all his relatives living in his house at the time) become compadres and comadres to the petitioners and their wives, thereby welding dozens of people into a ritual kin relationship. And the boy and girl begin to address the embracer and his wife as "father" and "mother." The embracer soon selects an old woman, who will serve as his consort during the wedding, since his wife is considered too young to serve.

After the boy and girl, accompanied by their families, the embracer, and his consort, have presented themselves to the Catholic priest and the banns have been read, preparations are made for the wedding at the boy's house. The boy's family must appoint a number of additional assistants: a ritual advisor, who will serve as master of ceremonies; two men to dance while the bean tamales are being cooked; a "bearer of flowers," who distributes orange branches and geraniums to all who dance at the wedding; two women to make the bean tamales; two men who supervise the butchering of the beef; and three musicians—a violinist, harpist, and guitarist. The girl's family has to provide only one additional person: "mother of the girl," who ritually takes the place of the bride's mother; she helps the bride dress and accompanies her to both church and house wedding.

The wedding proceeds in three phases: a civil ceremony, a church ceremony, and finally the house ceremony. Early in the morning the embracer, his consort, the appointed "mother of the girl," and all the girl's family meet the boy's group in the Ceremonial Center. They go first to the Cabildo where the Secretary records the name of the bride and groom, and asks them to sign (or to thumbprint if they cannot write). Then the groom pays the Secretary the civil marriage fee in pesos, and is given a slip of paper stating that he and his wife have been married by the civil authorities. In the afternoon the couple present themselves to the Catholic priest and give him the slip of paper from the Secretary. He also records their names and collects a fee for the church ceremony. Then he sends them to a lay sister for instruction on the catechism.

The following morning the bride and groom arise very early in order to be dressed and at the church by 5 a.m. The groom usually goes to the bride's house; alternatively, both may meet at the embracer's house and dress there. Both are clothed as elaborately as they will ever be in their lives. Standing on a bull-hide mat, the groom puts on a pair of knee-length, white cotton pants; then over his usual shirt, a long-sleeved white cotton shirt that comes to his waist. His outer clothing includes knee-length green velvet pants, a strip of white cloth that serves as a wide belt, a square piece of white cloth bordered with lace, and two red turbans wound around his head and neck. He carries a wide-brimmed, black felt hat, and looks like an Alferez in the cargo system who is about to go through a change of office ceremony (see Chapter 7).

The bride wears a new blouse and skirt, covered with a long white *huipil* embroidered with white chicken feathers. Her hair is done up with a long cloth strip of two colors, and then covered with a red scarf. She wears a large square of white cloth as a shawl in such a way as practically to cover her face and come below her hips. Rosaries and scapularies are placed around the necks of both the bride and groom.

At 5 a.m. the church bells ring and all the couples to be married that day arrive at the church of San Lorenzo. The groom leads the wedding party, followed by the embracer; then the bride enters, followed by the embracer's consort and the "mother of the girl." The bride and the groom kneel at the altar rail while the others sit on the first bench behind. The embracer lights candles, giving one each to bride and groom, one to his consort, and retaining one for himself. A lay sister collects coins and rings from the embracer. The priest arrives, takes a pink ribbon, makes a knot in it and slips it over the heads of the couple. Then he takes the thirteen coins and gives them to the groom, who in turn presents them to the bride saying (in Tzotzil) "I give you this money, wife," and she replies "I receive it, husband." (This is the first time they address each other as husband and wife.) The bride does not keep the coins, but lets them run through her fingers onto a plate held by the priest's helper. The money is kept by the church. Next the priest places one of the two rings on the groom's finger and gives him the other to place on the bride. The rings are kept until three days after the ceremony, when they are returned to the embracer, who has borrowed them. Then the priest says mass, gives communion to all the couples being married, and provides a short sermon on the responsibilities of marriage.

Following the ceremony, the wedding party files out and drinks a bottle of rum liquor outside the church. They then proceed to the house of the groom for the last phase of the wedding. All are inside the house, except for the ritual advisor, who meets them in the patio. The bride and groom stand hand in hand before the decorated house cross in the fumes of the burning copal incense. A table for a ritual meal is set up, with the ritual advisor seated at the head (east end), and bride and groom in the middle facing each other. They are flanked by the bride's adult male relatives and the embracer. At the foot of the table are the embracer's consort and the "mother of the girl." The groom's family proceeds to serve the meal. The bride and groom do not eat, but give their food to the embracer and his consort.

Following the meal, the embracer and his consort take the bride and groom into the house to remove their wedding clothes. This entrance marks the bride's introduction to her new home and her new relatives. She is now genuinely a married woman; if she leaves the boy now, her father will not have to repay him for all the money he spent on the courtship. The boy and girl are dressed in ceremonial robes, which symbolize their new adult status. The embracer gives them a lecture, telling the groom to work hard, to provide for his wife, and not to beat her; he tells the bride to obey her husband, to give him food when he is hungry, to get up early in the morning, and not be lazy. He also tells the groom's mother to be kind to her new daughter-in-law.

The embracer then has the musicians start playing and invites the bride's family into the house where they greet the groom's family. The groom's family serve them rum liquor, and the bride's family invite them outside to dance. The dancers form two lines: men in front and women behind, with the groom's mother holding the hand of the bride's mother as they dance. Meanwhile, the embracer and his consort dance around the whole group in a circle, with the consort following behind the embracer. Drinks are continually served, and as the dancing proceeds, more and more people drop in drunken stupors, until finally there are no dancers left.

The embracer and his consort go back inside the house to remove the ceremonial robes from the bride and groom and undo the bride's hair. The bride is then seated in front of a metate and told to grind corn. She is also shown the fire on which she will cook. The musicians leave, and the bride's family and helpers follow soon afterwards. Those who are drunk stay until the next morning. Meanwhile, the bride and groom spend the night among a group of drunken, sleeping relatives, often not consummating the marriage until the second night.

This description outlines the preferred type of courtship and marriage, but in fact many Zinacantecos cannot afford these expensive procedures and are forced to marry in other ways: by reducing the length of courtship and hence the amount of bride price; by treating the "house entering" ceremony as the wedding; or by an elopement, after which the boy must ask the pardon of the girl's parents and the boy's family still must pay the girl's family, though not as much as if they had been married "properly." This pattern of elopement has become more common as increased numbers of Zinacantecos can utilize money earned in wage work to compensate the girl's family in a kind of abbreviated payment of bride price.

Courtships may also be broken off, but when they are, the boy's family always demands the repayment of the money that has been spent, and the case usually goes to the Cabildo for negotiation. Divorce is also possible, and can be obtained at the Cabildo with an appropriate payment of pesos. For this sum, the Secretary simply erases his records, so that, from a "legal" point of view, the marriage never existed. In these cases, the church is never consulted, and the individuals feel free to remarry.

But generally the long courtship and various marriage ceremonies act to perpetuate Zinacanteco social structure, to create a stable marriage, and to prepare the new bride and groom for responsible adult roles. During the period of gift-giving the boy is symbolically providing for a woman, weaning her away from her own domestic group and into a relationship with himself and his family. The gifts also pay her father for the expenses of rearing her and thereby remove all of her family's claim over her services and her child-bearing potential. The children that are born later will take the two names of the husband's patriline and become members of his patrilineage.

At the house entering ceremony the boy is considered to have fulfilled the major part of his obligations. The time has come for him to become a member of the girl's family. The change is symbolized in part by the gifts: instead of luxury items like fruit, bread, and meat, he brings corn and beans, the staples of the Zinacanteco diet, and a blanket, symbolizing the sexual aspect of marriage.

In the minds of the Zinacantecos, the marriage actually takes place on two levels. Not only is an interaction set up between two groups of people, but also between the "inner souls" of the bride and groom. These souls are symbolically placed in the care of the embracer who is asked to plant them ("as pines and candles") firmly beneath the feet of the two important patron saints—San Lorenzo and Santo Domingo. This action is symbolized by the carrying of candles during the marriage ceremony in the church. After the wedding the embracer has the duty of keeping both the souls and the bodies of the bride and groom together by mediating any disputes that might threaten the marriage.

In the final stages of the wedding ceremony personal relationships are replaced by ritual ones. The "mother of the girl" replaces her mother, and the ritual advisor replaces her father. The ritual is thus in the hands of people who have little emotional commitment; the final separation of the girl from her family is achieved and she is successfully installed in the new household.

The events in Zinacanteco courtship and marriage provide a dramatic enactment of what Marcel Mauss has called "the system of total prestation"— an exchange of individuals, goods, services, courtesies, entertainment, and ritual, which is at once economic, social, religious, and moral. The reciprocal transactions that take place between the boy's and girl's families gradually bind the two groups to each other. Each family becomes more heavily committed, emotionally as well as financially. The boy's family invests more and more money and becomes increasingly interested in the outcome of the investment. The girl's family accepts more and more consumable goods that would be difficult to return if the courtship were to end. But even at an advanced stage, the girl's father is not entirely committed to giving away his daughter. It is only at the house entering ceremony that he makes the final transaction and accepts the boy into his house and family. Then, persons who play ritual roles take over and carry the courtship to completion. At the end, the bride's father is given no chance to break the bargain. The ritual continues until the bride is safely installed in her husband's home, and the bride and groom are planted together as firmly as two candles beneath the feet of San Lorenzo.

SERVING IN THE CARGO SYSTEM

Following his wedding, a young Zinacanteco ordinarily has to work diligently for a few years not only to provide for his new family, but also to pay off the debts incurred by his marriage. He and his wife also look forward to having a house of their own, a stage usually achieved by the time he is about twenty-five. Between about twenty-five and thirty he can begin to think about serving in the cargo system in the Ceremonial Center. He may serve on the school committee or be selected as one of the *Principales* to represent his *paraje* in the Center, but although these positions are increasing in number and importance in the hamlets, they do not give him the status and prestige that comes from serving in cargos in the ceremonial ladder.

When a Zinacanteco calculates that he will be ready for his first cargo some years in the future, he takes a bottle of liquor to present to *Moletik*

("Elders") on August 8th. On this date each year the *Moletik* sit outside the wall of the church of San Lorenzo and receive requests for cargos. The "waiting lists" are kept by the Scribes in hardcover notebooks that have a page or two devoted to each year in the future for which there is a cargo requested. The first man to appear with his bottle and request a particular cargo for a given year has his name recorded for that date. A man might, for example, request in 1988 the cargo of Senior Mayordomo Rey for 1998, only to be told that 1998 is already taken and that he may have the position in 2006. Alternatively, if he wishes to accept a less prestigeful cargo, such as the Junior Mayordomo of San Sebastián, he may be able to have the year 1998.

Once his name is recorded in the sacred book, he must reappear each August 8th, present another bottle of liquor, and reaffirm his intention to serve. If he does not appear, his name will be crossed out and the post will be given to another man. After the names are recorded, the book is kept by the Big Alcalde on his house altar. When the Alcalde leaves office at the end of the year, a complete copy is made in a new book to be kept by the incoming Alcalde and the outgoing Alcalde takes the copy of the lists used during his incumbency with him back to his paraje and keeps it in his house. This system is a strong check against tampering with the lists, because they can always be checked with past cargoholders in the hamlets.

As soon as a Zinacanteco has his name on the waiting lists, he acquires new prestige in the eyes of the community. He may not in fact serve for fifteen or twenty years, while he is waiting and preparing for the cargo, but it is widely known that he has made the crucial move of requesting the cargo and this defines him as a man of respect who is helping to carry on an important Zinacanteco tradition.

The costs of serving cargos vary from a few thousand pesos for the lowly Mayor, who serves as errand boy and policeman for the Cabildo, to more than a million pesos for the Senior Mayordomo Rey. These costs and the traditional rank determine the prestige a man derives from serving in a cargo. Since both the costs and the traditional ranks of cargos are public knowledge, cargos are clear ways of communicating the abilities and image of a man to his fellow Zinacantecos.

There are a number of ways of passing through the ceremonial ladder. A wealthy and ambitious Zinacanteco plans his strategy to serve four prestigious positions, perhaps the Senior Mayordomo Rey, the Alferez of Santo Domingo, the Regidor No. 1, and the Big Alcalde, or to come as close to this ideal as possible. A poorer Zinacanteco may aspire only to the lower cargos at each level and be satisfied by finishing as the Little Alcalde. And many Zinacantecos never serve more than one or two cargos before they either retire from the ranks or die. For although the numbers of cargos counting for service in the ladder in Zinacantan Center are slowly increasing, the population has undergone a dramatic increase in recent decades.

To achieve the ideal state of passing through the ladder at the highest prestige level depends not upon inherited land or money *per se*, but upon the successful manipulation and management of one's economic and social life. The resources needed to pay for the liquor, food, candles, and fireworks for a cargo costing at least ten times the annual income of a relatively prosperous Zinacanteco require that a man get on well with his kinsmen, and that he be called upon to serve as godparent for many baptisms and as a ritual official in many weddings so that he will have many ritual kinsmen to help him as well. This process tends to be circular: a respected man who has served in one or two cargos is more likely to be asked to serve as a godparent or as a ritual specialist in a wedding and thereby acquire more compadres. With the aid of the compadres, he is able to muster more people to help him with his next cargo. In turn, he then becomes more sought after to serve in more baptisms and weddings and acquire still more compadres; and so on.

Good management for a career in the cargo system also requires that a Zinacanteco be expert not only in maize-farming by his own efforts, but that he can become an entrepreneur in managing lands he acquires or trucks he purchases. He will need to call upon his kinsmen, including his compadres, not only for assistance in his maize-farming and/or in his trucking enterprises, but also as helpers when he serves in cargo positions. Even if he is a successful entrepreneur in farming or trucking, he will still have to borrow large sums of money in order to meet the expenses of cargos. Again, his kinsmen are basically the ones to whom he will turn for loans of cash.

Even with all these resources, a cargoholder ordinarily leaves office with a series of debts, and it takes some years before he has recouped his resources enough for assuming another cargo. In short, the "rest periods" between cargos are necessary not only to provide time for other men to serve, but also to provide each cargoholder with time to recover from the last cargo and get ready for the next one.

A major share of a Zinacanteco's energy and resources in his mature years (from about twenty-five to sixty-five) goes into planning for, serving in, and recovering from the four years of ceremonial duty he puts into performing rituals in the cargo system in Zinacantan Center. With some good fortune (such as the death of men ahead of him on the waiting lists), he can become an honored *pasado* ("emeritus") in his late years. If he has also managed to produce a large family to take over his lands and his house and to carry on his lineage, he has had a successful career. Now, he is no longer expected to serve in arduous ritual positions, although he is still called upon to give advice and to serve as a ritual advisor for other cargoholders as well as in weddings. But he no longer has to make contributions for fiestas when the Regidores come by collecting from heads of families. All the younger men bow to him, and accord him the respect due his age and his record of accomplishment. His wife, who has dutifully made his tortillas, directed his household, and helped him with his cargos all these years, is likewise accorded respect and is also called upon to help with domestic ceremonies.

DEATH

In Zinacanteco belief, no death, even for the very old, results from natural illness in the way in which we consider the process physiologically. Rather, death results from "soul loss," by having one's animal spirit companion let out of its corral, or by having one's "inner soul" sold irrevocably to the Earth-Owner. Or death may result from physical injury.

Most Zinacantecos die on their reed sleeping mats on the earthen floor of their homes. When death comes, the kerchief of a man, or shawl of a woman, is used to cover the face of the deceased. An older man or woman is called upon to bathe the corpse and dress it in clean clothes. The corpse is then put in a pine coffin purchased from Ladino carpenters. The head is placed to the West, and a chicken head is put in a bowl of broth beside the head of the corpse, along with some tortillas. The chicken allegedly leads the "inner soul" of the deceased to *Vinahel*. A black dog carries the "soul" across a river, and the tortillas compensate the dog for his assistance. Three small bags of money are placed with the body, two of them hidden at the sides so that they will not be stolen by the other "souls" upon arrival in *Vinahel*. At the foot, a small bowl and a gourd with water provide the necessary drinking implements, and a sack of charred tortillas for food is provided for the "soul" on its journey. Candles are lighted, musicians (violin, harp, guitar) play, and there is an all-night wake for the deceased.

At dawn a ritual meal is served, and preparations are made for the trip to the cemetery. All in the house cry openly to express their grief. The coffin is closed and carried outside, where it is fastened to two long poles that will rest on the shoulders of the four pall-bearers who carry it to the cemetery. Since the "soul" of the deceased wishes to take its family, friends, and possessions along, an important ritual act is performed to protect the survivors. The widow (or widower) spits salt water on the spot where the coffin was located during the wake and at all places around the house and patio where the deceased has worked, walked, and slept during his life.

To the accompaniment of loud wailing, the procession now forms, led by the musicians, and proceeds to the cemetery. It stops at specified places along the trail, where the coffin is opened, candles are lighted, prayers are said, and an old woman gives water to the corpse by sprinkling it on the lips with a geranium.

Upon arrival at the cemetery, the coffin is set down and the grave is dug. About every half hour, the deceased is given another "drink" with a red geranium (dipped in water) to relieve his thirst. The children who are present step up to the open coffin and kick the side of the coffin so that the deceased will not take their "souls" with him.

After a final round of prayers, the coffin is closed for the last time, and lowered halfway into the grave. A round of liquor is served, then the coffin is then lowered all the way, and all present come forward to throw three handfuls of dirt over the coffin to prevent the deceased from taking their "souls." The hat and high-backed sandals of a man are buried above the coffin, but the black bands in the hat are ripped and the "ears" of the sandals are cut—to prevent them from turning into snakes and bull horns. The grave is then completely filled. Fresh pine needles are placed over the grave, a small wooden cross is erected at the head (the corpse is buried with its head to the West), and candles are lighted—two white wax and one tallow—in the pit at the head of the grave. The white candles represent tortillas for the "soul" of the deceased; the tallow candle symbolizes meat.

Interaction with the dead by no means ceases after burial takes place. The close survivors make daily trips to the cemetery for nine days thereafter, following the Catholic "novena." Candles are lighted and prayers are said. In addition, special rituals are performed on *Todos Santos*, when the graves of all remembered deceased relatives are decorated with fresh pine needles (on the mounds), and pinetree tops and red geraniums (on the crosses). The graves are also decorated, prayers said, and candles offered on each important ceremonial occasion, such as the Fiestas of San Lorenzo and San Sebastián. By these ritual means the "inner soul" of the deceased continues to participate in the fiestas he enjoyed so much during his lifetime.

7/The Ritual Cycle

The Zinacanteco way of life emphasizes ceremony. Hardly a day passes in Zinacantan Center without some ritual being performed as the annual ceremonial calendar unfolds; hardly a week passes, even in the smaller hamlets, without at least one ceremony being performed by a shaman to cure illness, dedicate a new house, or offer candles in a maize field.

THE CEREMONIES OF THE CARGOHOLDERS

The complex and colorful ceremonies performed by the cargoholders in Zinacantan Center (see Early 1965) are scheduled by an annual ceremonial calendar that now coincides closely with the calendar of Catholic Saints' Days (see Table 7-1). On the seven most important Saints' days (indicated by asterisks in Table 7-1) there are major ceremonies that last three "official" days and involve repetitive ritual sequences to renew the flower decorations for the house altars and the churches, place sacred necklaces on the saint images, install incoming cargoholders and remove outgoing cargoholders, provide processions and dances, and feed all the cargoholders and their assistants special food and rum.

The Zinacantecos consider a "fiesta" (*k'in* in Tzotzil) for a particular saint to be of three days' duration, with the last day falling on the saint's day in the Catholic calendar. The first day is called what may be translated as "tying the flowers in bunches," the second "vespers," and the third "looking at the fiesta."

Three days of preparation precede the actual fiesta. Assistants are sent to San Cristobal to purchase candles, fireworks, liquor, meat, coffee, and rolls. For three nights before the first day, each Alférez who is about to leave his cargo (two Alféreces are changed at each major fiesta) sends out a party of assistants to announce the forthcoming fiesta. The party, consisting of a flautist, two drummers, and a drink-pourer, makes a circuit around the Ceremonial Center just after dark, and again just before dawn, playing special rhythmic fiesta-announcement music. They stop for rounds of liquor at certain cross shrines in the streets and at the doorways of the churches, and then return to the house of the Alférez for more liquor.

On the day before the official "first day," all of the Mayordomos put on

TABLE 7-1   THE ANNUAL CEREMONIAL CALENDAR
(MAJOR FIESTAS ARE MARKED WITH AN ASTERISK)

December 30	Cargo change for the Mayordomos Reyes, Mesoneros,
—January 1:	Escribanos, Regidores, and Alcaldes Viejos.
January 6:	Epifanía.
January 15:	Señor de Esquipulas.
* January 20:	San Sebastián.
February 2:	Virgen de Candelaria.
The Easter Season:	(Movable dates, dependent upon the date of Easter Sunday in any given year.)
	Carnaval: The five days preceding Ash Wednesday.
	Miércoles de Ceniza.
	Los Seis Viernes.
	Domingo de Ramos.
	Semana Santa.
	Pascua de Resurrección.
	Ascención del Señor.
	Venida del Espíritu Santo.
	* Santísima Trinidad.
	Sagrado Corazón de Jesús.
* April 29:	San Pedro Mártir.
May 3:	Santa Cruz.
June 13:	San Antonio.
June 24:	San Juan.
June 29:	San Pedro.
August 4:	Santo Domingo.
* August 10:	San Lorenzo.
August 31:	Santa Rosa.
* September 8:	Virgen de Natividad.
September 21:	San Mateo.
* October:	Sunday before October 7 the fiesta for the Virgen del Rosario is celebrated in Zinacantan.
October 7:	Fiesta for the Virgen del Rosario is celebrated in Salinas.
October 18:	San Lucas.
November 1:	Todos Santos.
November 25:	Santa Catalina.
December 8:	Purísima Concepción de María Santísima.
December 12:	Virgen de Guadalupe.
December 25:	Navidad.

their black ceremonial robes, and—to the music of a violin, harp, and guitar, and assisted by two old women past menopause who serve as Incense Bearers—renew the flower decorations on their respective house altars. They first pray to the musicians, chanting:

> See then, my older brother
> See then, my younger brother
>   In your presence,
>   Before your eyes,
>   We will change the flowers,

Photo 12. A ritual procession preceded by the guitar, harp, and violin players. (Photo by Frank Cancian)

> We will change the leaves of the tree,
> Of Father San Lorenzo,
> Of Father Santo Domingo. . . .

Then the two Incense Bearers kneel at the edge of a reed mat in front of the altar, each with a smoking censer, while the Mayordomos remove the dry geraniums and leaves from an arch over the altar and throw them on the mat. Assistants bring in fresh geranium blossoms and green leaves, which the Incense Bearers tie into small bouquets and hand to the Mayordomos, who tie them on the arch with a cord, making a beautiful new decoration.

Then the small saint images kept on the altars are dressed in freshly washed and incensed clothes, and candles are lighted as "food for the saints." They kneel and pray:

> The changing of the flowers is finished,
> The changing of the leaves of your tree is done.
>
> Now we have arrived at your great feast day,
> Now we have arrived at your great festival. . . .
>
> You will be entertained,
> You will be happy,
> On your great feast day,
> On your great festival.
>
> So receive my candle, my father,
> So receive my candle, my lord. . . .

The Mayordomos and Incense Bearers then dance and sing for an hour to special tunes for the entertainment of the saints on the altar.

While the Mayordomos are renewing the flower decorations on their house altars, the Alféreces are participating in the oath of office ceremony for the two new incumbents entering their year of cargo service. This ceremony takes place in the Hermitage of Esquipulas where the saint Señor Esquipulas is wearing his sacred necklace, and the Alcaldes Viejos, the Scribes, and a delegation of officials from the Cabildo are all seated at the long center table. The batons of the Alcaldes are on the table, with their silver heads pointed toward the foot of the table, to receive the new Alféreces. The first new Alférez arrives with his escorting party, consisting of the four Regidores, flute and drum players and fireworks specialists, as well as family members. The Regidor who has been carrying the black hat (with peacock feather) of the new Alférez delivers it to the Big Alcalde. The new Alférez then enters, genuflects, and walks to the foot of table. Then in order of seniority, each of the seated officials rises and delivers this exhortation:

> You have come to receive,
> You have come to take,
> The holy divine oath,
> Here before the feet,
> Here before the hands,

> Of the Lord Esquipulas,
>> Oh my venerable father. . . .

You must be a good servant,
You must be faithful to your trust,
> You must leave the cargo in order,
> You must leave the cargo prepared,
>> For the two who will succeed you,
>> For your two successors,
>>> For a year in the divine world,
>>> During a year on the divine earth,
>>>> Oh my venerable father. . . .

The incoming Alférez then moves closer to the foot of table and puts his head on the table between his hands. The Big Alcalde rises, comes to foot of table and intones the oath:

> He came to receive,
> He came to take,
>> The holy, divine oath
>>> Here under your feet,
>>> Here under your hands. . . .

He must be a good person,
He must be faithful to his trust,
> For twelve months,
> For twelve days,
>> Here under your feet,
>> Here under your hands. . . .

May he keep in sight,
May he keep before his eyes,
> His cargo,
> His service. . . .

The Alcalde makes the sign of the cross over the bowed head of the Alférez who rises and lights a candle at the altar of Señor Esquipulas. He is then handed his black hat, his Ritual Advisor comes forward to tie the red turban around his head, and the Big Alcalde reverses the direction of one of the batons on the table so that the silver head points toward the oath-taker at the head of the table. The new Alférez then serves a round of liquor, rolls, and coffee to all present, and sits with the other seated officials to await the arrival of the second Alférez being sworn in at this fiesta.

On the first "official" day of the fiesta, the Mayordomos renew the flower decorations in the two churches of San Lorenzo and San Sebastián. The twelve Mayordomos, accompanied by their three musicians and their assistants, meet in front of the church of San Lorenzo. They dress in their black ceremonial robes and file into the church in rank order. The ritual of renewing the flowers follows almost the same pattern as the house altar flower change the night before. The old flowers are removed, and fresh flowers are placed on the arches above each of the saint images. Fresh pine needles are placed on the floor, then candles are lighted as "food for the saints." The Mayordomos pray, and later dance on a patio in front of the church for the entertainment of the saints. In the afternoon the performance is repeated for the saints in the church of San Sebastián.

In the late afternoon the Mayordomos return to the church of San Lorenzo where they are joined by all the other cargoholders, except for the Alféreces who are waiting to offer hospitality to the officials at the house of the more senior Alférez who is leaving his cargo. A procession forms in the churchyard and the cargoholders march to the house of the Alférez, where they are ritually received and seated in rank order. Here they are each offered a shot of rum liquor and a gourd of coffee with two rolls on top covered with a napkin. They then all proceed to the house of the junior outgoing Alférez where the sequence is repeated. This late afternoon ritual on the first day is the first of two farewell gestures offered to the cargoholders by the Alféreces who are leaving their cargos.

The Alféreces then spend the night in a standard ceremonial circuit that is repeated on the second and third nights of the fiesta. The retinue of flute and drum players proceeds to the house of the second musician, the guitar player, where they are served a meal. They "pick-up" the guitar player and proceed to the house of the first musician, the violin player, where they are served another meal. They then pick up the violinist and proceed to the house of the Alférez of San Lorenzo, where they are served liquor and dance to the violin and guitar music in honor of San Lorenzo. And so on through the night until they have picked up all fourteen Alféreces and have been served at least liquor, and often rolls or *atole*, at each of the houses. Finally, at the last house they stay to rest until dawn.

On the morning of the second day of the fiesta, the Alféreces perform "the dance of the drunks." Leaving the house where they spent the night, they march to the church of San Lorenzo. After praying to the saints, they sit on long benches on the terrace in front of the church—the seven senior Alféreces separated from the seven junior Alféreces by the violin and guitar players. The two Alféreces leaving office and the two entering office are dressed in special costumes: green or blue velvet breeches, red knee socks, blue capes, and gorgeous peacock feathers in their large black hats. They rise and initiate "the dance of the drunks," a highly stylized, humorous dance in which they shake their rattles, and periodically yell, leap, and change places. As the dance progresses, they act as if they are becoming drunker and drunker, their movements becoming more erratic. They end the dance by collapsing in "drunken stupors" beside the lined-up liquor bottles and taking great gulps of rum liquor. Later they are joined by the other Alféreces, all of whom perform the dance. During one of the rests, the two outgoing Alféreces pass down the line of seated Alféreces, offering drinks of liquor and apologizing, often crying, for any defects in the manner they have performed their cargos during the year. This "dance of the drunks" reflects in both its ritual behavior and its mood the deep sense of ambivalence the Alféreces feel about their cargos. For while cargo-holding brings great prestige and an exciting life in the Ceremonial Center, it also brings great expenses and subsequent debts that will take years to repay (Vogt 1976).

Meanwhile the Mayordomos have assembled and are dancing for the saints inside the church of San Lorenzo. Later they move to their benches outside on the terrace and engage in reciprocal drinking while they watch the Alféreces dance.

The afternoon of the second day is highlighted by a ritual sequence in which the outgoing Alféreces serve *atole* to all the cargoholders. Again, the party marches in rank order first to the house of the outgoing Senior Alférez and then to the house of the outgoing Junior Alférez. In each house they are served first liquor and then two generous servings of the sweet corn gruel.

During the second night the Alféreces repeat their ceremonial circuit of making the rounds of all the Alféreces' houses where they drink and dance. The Mayordomos have a more special ritual to perform: to count the sacred necklaces of the saints and then take them to the churches and place them around the necks of the images. These necklaces, consisting of a series of ancient and modern coins suspended from a wide, red silk ribbon, are kept carefully stored in bundles inside the chests the Mayordomos keep on their house altars, and transferred at the end of their year of cargo duty to the incoming Mayordomos. On major fiestas the necklaces are removed from the chests, counted, and then taken to the churches and placed on the saint images. After the fiesta, they are removed and returned to their chests in the Mayordomos' houses.

This ritual sequence begins about two hours after sunset when each pair of Mayordomos assembles with his assistants, including the two Incense Bearers and the Sacristans, at the house of the Senior member of the pair, where the chest is kept. The bundle is removed from the locked chest, held over smoking incense, and then opened. The necklaces are removed and placed on a reed mat. The Senior Mayordomo holds one end of the red ribbon, and the Junior Mayordomo the other end. The Senior Mayordomo counts the value of the coins, moving them one at a time, while a Sacristan moves kernels of maize to record the count. (Unschooled Zinacantecos cannot add except by moving grains of maize and then counting the pile of maize at the end.) Each necklace has a matching bag of maize kernels, supposedly equal to the value of the coins, which is also kept in the chest. The count usually varies each time it is made, sometimes coming out higher (that is, more value in coins than number of maize kernels), and sometimes lower. The belief is that when the count is higher the saint is pleased with the services of his Mayordomo and rewards him by miraculously adding coins to the necklace. When the count is lower, the saint is punishing the Mayordomo for poor performance (see Renato Rosaldo 1968).

At about 2 A.M. each pair of Mayordomos sets out for the church, with an assistant carrying a smoking censer and a pine torch, and the three musicians playing. The Senior Mayordomo carries the necklaces in a fold of his black ceremonial robe. After all the necklaces are placed on the proper images, the Mayordomos dance from 3 to about 7 A.M. in front of the various images in the two churches.

On the third day of the fiesta, the Catholic priest arrives from San Cristobal in the early morning to perform marriages and baptisms and to say Mass. The priest ordinarily leaves by 10 A.M. as the church bell signals his departure. Then the Alféreces repeat their "dance of the drunks," while the Mayordomos dance inside the church for the saints.

About noon the Mayordomos remove the sacred necklaces from the saints and return them to the chests on the altars in their houses, where they will remain until the next major fiesta. (A similar ritual is performed by the Mayordomos Reyes and Mesoneros who must count the necklaces and place them on the image of Señor Esquipulas in the Hermitage not only for each major fiesta, but every Sunday of the year.)

The final ritual in a major three day ceremony takes place on the afternoon of the third day—the transfer of red flags from the two outgoing Alféreces to the two incoming Alféreces. This ritual takes place in front of the Hermitage of Esquipulas, with all of the cargoholders and the civil officials participating. Using two flags borrowed from the Mayordomos, the two outgoing Alféreces crawl on their knees to meet the two senior Regidores, who are also crawling on their knees. They kiss each other's necklaces and then the Alféreces hand the flags to the Regidores, saying:

> My venerable father,
> > Before your sight,
> > Before your eyes,
> > > The holy divine banner,
> > > > Is going to leave my feet,
> > > > Is going to leave my hands,
> > > > > Oh my venerable father.

> Now the time is passed,
> Now the hour is passed. . . .

> It alone did I watch,
> It alone did I have before my eyes,
> > My cargo,
> > My cargo,
> In the same way they must watch,
> In the same way they must have before their eyes,
> During a year in the divine world,
> During a year on the divine earth,
> > The two who follow me,
> > My two successors. . . .

The two incoming Alféreces then kneel and crawl forward to receive the two red flags as a symbol that they have taken over their new cargo. The whole hierarchy then proceeds first to the house of the Big Alcalde and then the Little Alcalde's for a round of liquor and *atole*.

In addition to the constantly repeating ritual sequences just described, there are five occasions during the year—Christmas-New Year, San Sebastián in January, Easter, San Lorenzo in August, and Virgen del Rosario in October—when the cargoholders perform special ceremonies with very distinctive rituals as complicated and interesting as any that occur in the Highlands of Chiapas today.

CHRISTMAS-NEW YEAR

This is a period of elaborate ritual combining the period of Christmas (the Virgen de Navidad celebration days of December 15 to 25, the *octavo* which follows, and the Day of Kings on January 6) with a dance drama that begins on December 24 and ends on January 6. During the days of December 30 through January 1, there are also change-of-cargo rituals for the Alcaldes Viejos, the Regidores, and the Mayores.

The ritual sequence begins with a flower renewal by the Mayordomos in their houses and in the churches. There follows a period of nine days (December 16 to 24) when the Mayordomos gather in front of the church of San Lorenzo each morning and eat sweetened squash to commemorate the nine months of the Virgin's pregnancy. During the same period the Mayordomos and Sacristans perform the *posada* (inn) ceremony to commemorate the narrative of Joseph and Mary seeking lodging at many inns before the birth of the Christ child.

On December 23 the Mayordomos and their assistants construct an enormous, beautiful crèche in the church of San Lorenzo. The corners of the crèche are large, freshly cut pine trees, and the walls and roof are made of pine boughs. The edges of the walls and roof are decorated with streamers of red, white, and orange flowers, and the crib is placed inside.

On December 24 a reed mat "bull" is constructed, which will become the focus of dancing and fun-making in the dance drama. The "bull" is carried over the head and shoulders of a man, and it performs with two married couples (the males are masked and ride stick horses, while their spouses are unmasked) impersonated by the Mayordomos (who take turns). The performance is watched by two young boys dressed as "angels." During the next twelve days the drama is repeated over and over: the "bull" attacks the husbands, while the wives lift their skirts to expose their genitalia in attempt to "tame" the "bull." Finally, the "bull" gores and kills the husbands, who are revived when their wives take them to a high official who rubs their bodies, especially their genitals, with the rattles they have been using in the dance (see Bricker 1973).

At midnight on Christmas Eve, the births of the Christ children (there are two in Zinacantan belief: one older brother and one younger brother) are re-enacted in the church of San Sebastián. The two children are carried by their godparents—the top civil officials from the Cabildo, i.e., the Presidente, the Síndico, the Jueces, and the Regidores—to the church of San

Lorenzo where they are placed in the crèche where all come forward to venerate them to the resonant sound of turtle shell drums.

The ritual sequence ends on January 6 with the chasing, capture, and killing of the "bull." The boy "angels," who have passively watched the drama up to this point, now lasso the "bull" and kill him with wooden knives plunged into his body. His "blood" (consisting of rum liquor with onions and chile to make it red) is passed around and drunk. This dance drama clearly expresses many of the lines of tension in Zinacanteco life (such as the relation between men and women, the relation between young and old, and the complex relationships between compadres); the "bull" appears to be a symbol of social disorder, which is eventually overcome and order restored as the "bull" is ritually killed.

SAN SEBASTIÁN

San Sebastián's day in the Catholic calendar is January 20, but this ceremony lasts nine days, from January 17, when the Mayordomos renew the flowers on their house altars, until January 25, when the Big Alcalde transfers sacred symbols of his authority to his successor. By all odds the most complex ceremony performed in Zinacantan, it has some unusual features, perhaps the most remarkable that the major costumed performers are the cargoholders who have "officially" finished their year of service but who must perform throughout this ceremony before they finish their duties. Thus, for example, the Alcaldes of the previous year become "Spanish Gentlemen" dressed in gold embroidered red coats and knickers; the two most senior Alféreces become "Spanish Ladies" wearing white embroidered blouses and carrying combs in small bowls; the Regidores become "White Heads" (also known as "Montezumas") with white hats, shirts, capes, and breeches, and "Lacandons" dressed in purple dress coats and breeches; two other Alféreces become "Jaguars" dressed in jaguar suits with tails; the Mayordomos Reyes become "Feathered Serpents"; others become "Spanish Moss Wearers," and "Blackmen." All in all, a most extraordinary collection of "celebrators" of the fiesta.

Sacred objects are brought into the Center from various hamlets: a small sacred drum that is played for some of the dances, a jousting target and a lance used for a jousting pantomime, and so on. The sequence of events includes the arrival of the Spanish Gentlemen and Ladies on horseback for the jousting pantomime and dancing; the "Blackmen" dancing with stuffed squirrels with which they engage in comic play, including simulating intercourse between the squirrels; the climbing of the "Jaguar Tree" and the ritual burning of the "Jaguar House"; two enormous ritual meals during which the entire hierarchy of cargoholders sits down to servings of whole chickens; the "Jaguars" performing a caricature of a curing ceremony, with one Jaguar impersonating a shaman and the other playing the role of his patient.

The ceremony finally ends on January 25 when the past year's cargoholders escort the outgoing Big Alcalde, with his articles of office, to the house of the incoming Big Alcalde. An elaborate ritual follows in which he hands over the sacred picture of San Sebastián, two candleholders, a box containing a stamp, a seal, and some papers, and the branding iron for Zinacantan.

This ceremony appears to have some slight connection with the myth of the slaying of San Sebastián as told in Catholic theology, but it has obviously developed an accretion of many additional complex elements. It is an "End-of-Year" ceremony with a riot of role-reversals and inversions which, like the second line of a couplet in a Tzotzil-Maya ritual prayer, restates and intensifies the themes that were introduced during the Christmas-New Year period (Vogt 1976). But the ceremony also provides an annual commentary on the history and structure of ethnic conflict in the Chiapas Highlands, with the appearance of Feathered Serpents, Montezumas, Spanish Conquerors, Lacandons, and Blackmen, as well as on the animal and plant world, with the appearance of Jaguars and Tree Mosses (Bricker 1981). Some of the sequences may even derive from the activities of the twins in the famous *Popul Vuh* (Dennis Tedlock 1985) or its equivalent narrative told by the ancestors of the Zinacantecos.

EASTER

Since Easter is a movable date in the Catholic calendar, the ritual sequence from Carnaval through Lent to Easter Sunday varies from year to year. The ritual for this period is focused around one saint, *Santo Entierro*, who is called "The Buyer" in Tzotzil. This is a very large image of a crucified Christ kept in the church of San Lorenzo. The theme for the season is the pursuit of "The Buyer" by demons and the death of "The Buyer" by crucifixion on Good Friday.

Carnaval is called "the fiesta of games" and it lasts a week, ending on the eve of Ash Wednesday. The most important performers are two *Pasioneros* who offer candles, dance, say prayers at cross shrines, and provide food and drink for other participants. Their ritual service continues through Holy Week when they portray two "Jews" and have the duty of guarding the bier of the crucified Christ and of stroking the image with flowers given them by the other cargoholders. Also active for Carnaval are an indefinite number of "Blackmen," impersonated by young Zinacantecos dressed as Ladinos, and the "Father Blackman," who blackens his face, wears an old black hat, shirt, breeches, an army coat, and an old patched blanket, and carries a bull's horn full of *chicha*. (This corn "beer" is especially fermented for Carnaval by the Zinacantecos.) These "Blackmen" drink *chicha*, make the rounds of all the cargoholders' houses where they are given liquor, and dance and recite *bombas*, short comical songs. The "Blackmen" represent the demons who later pursue "The Buyer."

Every Friday during Lent a procession forms inside the church of San Lorenzo and the crucified Christ image is taken in a slow circuit around the church. On the Fourth Friday, the procession is larger and goes out into the churchyard. On Monday of the Holy Week the Sacristans buy after-shave lotion in San Cristobal which they will use on Wednesday to wash the image. The washing is done by the Alcaldes and the six Holy Elders, six old men who occupy these positions on a permanent basis and whose major duty occurs during Holy Week. At noon on Good Friday the Alcaldes and the Holy Elders place the image on a large cross inside the church while the Sacristans sound wooden clappers and a choir chants Lenten hymns. From noon until 2 P.M. the church is thronged with Zinacantecos who come to bring candles and flowers and pray. Then by sundown the image is lowered and placed back in its bier. On Saturday the Mayordomos come to take down the cross and clean up the church. Easter Sunday resembles the third day of any fiesta with the Alféreces drinking and dancing their "dance of the drunks" in front of the church and being joined by the Mayordomos, who engage in reciprocal drinking and then all go off to the houses of outgoing Alferéces for *atole*.

SAN LORENZO

San Lorenzo's day is August 10, but this fiesta is for the patron saint of Zinacantan, and it lasts five days—from August 7, when the band arrives, vendors set up their stands in the market and the Mayordomos renew their house altar decorations, to August 11, when the saints that have been "visiting" from other villages return to their homes. While San Lorenzo is the patron saint, there is little distinctive ritual during this fiesta. Rather, the ritual sequence is like an expanded version of the three-day ceremony described above. The only distinctive additional performers are the *Capitanes*, who are costumed in brown skull caps from which red feathers dangle, rolled red turbans tied around their heads, and blue kerchiefs around their necks, plus everyday shirts under old, torn black suit jackets and blue or green breeches, which meet red stockings below the knees. They carry bright scarves in their right hands, and gold paint streaks their faces. They accompany the processions, meeting the six saints that visit from other villages and perform their dance at ritual stops and later at visits to cargoholders' houses throughout the fiesta. The dance is done by the Capitanes facing each other and making rhythmic hops on one foot while the other foot is extended in front off the ground. At intervals of a few minutes, the Capitanes throw their scarves over their shoulders with a shout and exchange places, now hopping on the foot that had been lifted, and extending the other foot. These Capitanes may be an image of the "one-legged hummingbird" mentioned in Zinacanteco mythical poetry (Hunt 1977).

Otherwise, the fiesta is noted for having the largest number of Zinacantecos, as well as residents of other villages, many of whom accompany the visiting saints that attend the fiesta. The fiesta comes at a period in the agricultural cycle when the heavy work of the second weeding in the cornfields has been finished and when both fresh corn and many fruits are available. I would estimate that more than 8000 people attend to watch the ceremonies,

Photo 13. During the fiesta of San Sebastián the Big Alcalde (of the previous year) impersonates a "Spanish Gentleman" and dances to violin, harp, and guitar music. (Photo by Frank Cancian)

especially the spectacular fireworks, and to trade in the market, where there is a brisk exchange of Highland and Lowland products.

VIRGEN DEL ROSARIO

The last fiesta of the year of special character and significance is the ceremony for the Virgen del Rosario, whose image is kept in the chapel in the hamlet of Salinas, or *'Ats'am* ("Salt"), where the sacred salt well is located. On the Sunday before October 7 (the actual day of this saint in the Catholic calendar), the image is brought from Salinas to Zinacantan Center, and a three-day major ceremony (of the type described above) takes place. Then the Mayordomos Reyes from Zinacantan Center together with their families and assistants accompany the image back to Salinas and perform a five-day ceremony there. The climax of the ceremony is a special offering to the sacred salt well. Each Mayordomo Rey prepares a special censer (especially made for this ceremony) with copal incense; the two burning censers are then lowered into the salt well and the top is covered over and wrapped up with reed mats. Then the Mayordomos Reyes and their wives dance (supposedly without stopping except to eat and drink rum) for three days and nights to pay homage to the Virgen del Rosario and her sacred salt well. During the ceremony other members of the hierarchy, including the Alcaldes, Regidores, and Mayordomos, also make a pilgrimage to Salinas to offer candles and pray. At the end, the exhausted Mayordomos Reyes and their wives and assistants return to Zinacantan with the assurance that the Virgen has been well entertained and will permit her salt to be brought to the Hermitage of Esquipulas and distributed to the cargoholders during the course of the year.

THE CEREMONIES OF THE SHAMANS

While the annual ceremonial round is unfolding in Zinacantan Center, the shamans are performing other kinds of ceremonies, mainly, but not exclusively, in the hamlets (see Fabrega and Silver 1973). Some shamans must of course perform needed ceremonies for those families living temporarily or permanently in the Ceremonial Center; and Year Renewal ceremonies (see below) are also performed in the Center.

The ceremonies regularly performed by the shamans include curing ceremonies, lineage and waterhole ceremonies (see Chapter 4), agricultural ceremonies (see Chapter 5), new house ceremonies, rain-making ceremonies, and Year Renewal ceremonies.

THE CURING CEREMONIES

Although there is no generic Tzotzil term for "curing ceremony," a number of behavior sequences and prayers focus upon a person who feels or has *chamel* ("sickness"). These include two types of divination called "pulsing" and "face of the maize." The pulsing procedure is used as a basic technique by all shamans to determine the cause of the illness. The shaman feels the pulse of the patient at the wrist and on the inside of the elbow, first on the right arm and then on the left arm. It is believed that the blood "talks" and provides messages that the shaman can understand and interpret.

Divining with "the face of the maize" involves the use of maize kernels to discover how many parts of the "inner soul" are missing in cases of soul-loss. The shaman used thirteen grains of maize in each of four colors—white, yellow, red, and black. The grains are thrown in sequence into a bowl of salt water—first white maize, then, in turn, yellow, red, and black. The shaman then inspects the fifty-two grains, counting how many are floating or "standing up" compared to the number resting on the bottom of the bowl. The number of floating grains indicates the number of lost parts of the "inner soul" of the patient.

The question of why fifty-two grains of maize are used when the soul is reported to have only thirteen parts has mystified us for several years. Informants are unclear why there is this apparent mathematical discrepancy. Several of us working in Zinacantan have observed the procedure many times, but by the time this divination is performed in the ritual sequence so much liquor has been consumed by the participants that the operational results are confused to say the least. The shaman, several of the assistants, and often the ethnographer as well, peer into the bowl of salt water trying to count the floating grains by the dim light of flashlights or flickering pine torches. After some discussion the shaman typically announces that five, six, or seven parts of the "inner soul" have been lost and proceeds with the ceremony. I suspect that we have here a remnant of an earlier belief that relates to some pattern of numeration or calendrical reckoning, or possibly to multiple "animal spirit companions." The latter is the most intriguing possibility, and I am currently working on the hypothesis that the Zinacantecos may formerly have believed that a person's "inner soul," with its thirteen parts, was shared with four "animal spirit companions" located in mountains in the four directions, and that these are represented by the white, yellow, red, and black colors of the maize—especially since these correspond with the traditional ancient Maya directional colors.

The ritual procedures and prayers also include a series of sequences that for our purposes may be called "curing ceremonies." We have had major difficulties eliciting a consistent set of these ceremonies. While the *public* ceremonies performed by both the cargoholders and the shamans (see below) are consistently labeled, the *private* curing ceremonies performed for domestic groups show a great deal of variation—both in procedure and in classification in the minds of the Zinacantecos. However, a basic distinction is made be-

Photo 14. During a curing ceremony the shaman pray to the Ancestral Gods to spare the life of the patient. From right, the shaman, the patient, and the husband of the patient. (Photo by Frank Cancian)

tween "good" and "bad" ceremonies. The "good" ceremonies are generally called "asking pardon," and they are differentiated from "bad" ceremonies, which are called "on account of witchcraft."

The class of "good" ceremonies includes:

1. "To say with words"—a very simple curing procedure, including a diagnosis by pulsing followed by a short prayer and either the rubbing of salt on the patient or boiling plants for the patient to drink or to have rubbed on his head. The ritual only takes about an hour. It is performed because an Ancestral God is angry with the patient for some minor infraction and has caused a headache, toothache, or other specific pain.
2. "He enters in the flowers" is a type of ceremony involving a ceremonial circuit of Zinacantan Center, a visit to one or more mountain shrines and churches, and the decoration of the patient's bed with flowers. In its most elaborate form it is called "the great vision" or alternatively "big flower." The "great vision" refers to the large number of gods that will be visited and "seen" in the mountain homes; the "big flower" to the large number of flower decorations that are required for the ceremony. It is performed to sustain the "animal spirit companion" of a patient, and is the longest, and most complex, curing ceremony. It may last between twenty-four and thirty-six hours or more. In shortened form, the ceremony is called "half flower," and is frequently performed when a patient cannot afford the full treatment.
3. "Asking pardon with candles" is essentially the same as (2) except that the patient's bed is not decorated.

"THE GREAT VISION"

For the largest, most complex "Great Vision" ceremony the Zinacantecos go through at least nineteen steps in the ritual. I shall summarize these briefly to provide something of the flavor of a curing ceremony (for more details see Vogt 1976).

1. The patient first seeks a shaman, who pulses him and determines both the nature of his illness and the ritual that will be necessary. The shaman indicates what ritual materials will be needed and a time is set for the ceremony.
2. The patient and his family make preparations, which involve recruiting four male assistants and four or more female assistants who assemble at the patient's house at dawn on the day of the ceremony. The male assistants set off immediately for Zinacantan Center to fetch a gourdful of water from each of the seven sacred waterholes. Then they gather the necessary plants in the woods for decorating the crosses, while all but three of the female assistants grind corn for tortillas. One woman goes to purchase red geraniums, and two go to Zinacantan Center to wash the patient's clothing in a special sacred waterhole. Two men are sent to San Cristobal to purchase candles, incense, chickens (if the family does not have enough), and rolls for the ceremony.

    When the men return with the plants, they go to "sweep" the cross shrines that will be visited. They remove the dried pine needles and replace them with fresh needles. Meanwhile, at home the family is constructing an enclosure around the patient's bed.

3. When all is ready, a male assistant goes to the shaman's house to fetch him, taking along a bottle of liquor and two rolls to request that he come.

4. When the shaman is about to arrive, two censers are lighted; one is placed at the foot of the house cross and the other at the foot of the table that has been oriented east-west inside the house. The shaman first stops at the house cross, then enters the house, kneels and prays at the table, and exchanges bowing and releasing gestures with everyone present. The moment the shaman enters, the male assistants become *Mayores* for the ceremony—that is, the equivalent of the errand boys who serve the Cabildo.

5. The shaman seats himself at the table and inspects the candles and other ritual materials to see if all is in order.

6. With the aid of the Mayores, the shaman censes and then assembles and ties together the bundles of plants for the patient's bed and for the mountain shrines. The bundles are placed around the bed and an arch is constructed over the entrance.

7. The shaman calls for a large pot and puts into it a small quantity of each type of plant, along with water from each of the seven sacred waterholes. The pot is placed on the fire to heat.

8. The shaman prays over the candles. The words he speaks are believed to be received by the gods at the moment he utters them. He prays:

> In the divine name of Jesus Christ my lord,
> So much my father,
> So much my lord,
> I beseech your divine pardon,
> I beg your divine permission,
> At the holy head of the table,
> At the holy foot of the table.
>
> Will you stand up in holiness,
> Will you stand firmly in holiness,
> Behind,
> Beside,
> Your sons,
> Your children,
> Your flowers,
> Your offspring,
> Who have sickness,
> Who have pain,
> Who are suffering,
> Who are miserable. . . .

In addition to the words, the gods will receive the candles, the liquor, and the meals that are served. After the shaman finishes, he calls forward each of the others to salute the candles.

9. The patient is then bathed by the shaman with water from the pot that has been heating. The women cense the newly washed clothing over an incense burner; these are put on by the patient after his bath.

10. One of the two black chickens is bathed in the same water. A vein in its throat is cut by the shaman, and into a bowl is drained about a cupful of blood, which the patient drinks. The wound is sewn up and the chicken is placed on a layer of

fresh pine needles on a plate, for it will later be killed and served to the angry gods at *Kalvaryo* as a "substitute" for the "inner soul" of the patient. The shaman then prepares the other ritual materials for the pilgrimage: the candles, pinetree tops, pine needles, bunches of plants, the chicken, bottles of liquor and food for the journey.

11. A ritual meal (see Chapter 8) is eaten by the shaman, the patient, the Mayores, and the women who washed the clothes.

12. The members of the curing party load for the trip, kneel, and cross themselves at the table, at the hearth, and then at the house cross. They march in rank order—the shaman in the rear, directly preceded by the patient, then the carrier of the candles; the others are out in front. One carries a kerosene lamp or pine pitch torches for the ceremony, which will extend through the long night. It may take two or three hours to reach the Ceremonial Center from their paraje, as they march up and down mountain trails.* Upon arrival in Zinacantan Center, they typically visit the following mountains: San Cristobal, *Mushul Vits*, Santa Cecilia, and finally *Kalvaryo*. The three Catholic churches are included in the circuit in passing. The sequence is identical at each mountain shrine, except for *Kalvaryo*: the Mayores prepare the crosses, attaching fresh pine tips and red geraniums and the other plants; the shaman prays and lights candles; the shaman and patient pray together; and rounds of liquor are served at fixed intervals. As the shaman "sees" the Ancestral God inside the mountain, he prays with such phrases as these:

> In the divine name of Jesus Christ my lord,
> > Take this, then, father
> > Receive this, then, lord
> > > Divine Maria Cecilia, my mother
> > > [name of sacred mountain]
> > > Divine Maria Cecilia, my lady.
>
> I come kneeling, then
> I come bowing low
> > At your lordly side
> > At your lordly front,
> > > Receive this, and
> > > Let me step
> > > Let me walk
> > > > To the descents of your feet [ritual
> > > > terms referring to mountain shrines]
> > > > To the descents of your hands.
>
> You who are thought,
> You who are measurement,
> > If you will stand up in holiness,
> > If you will stand firmly in holiness,
> > > Receive, then, at your holy back
> > Receive, then, at your holy side,

* I have yet to observe a case where the patient is too ill to make this pilgrimage. But in the event that a patient cannot make the journey, my Zinacanteco informants report that the shaman will either omit this part of the ceremony, or may ask that the clothes of the patient be taken to symbolically represent him.

Your sons
Your children
Your flowers
Your sprouts.

If you will accept this graciously,
If you will think well of me,
This lowly little bit
This humble amount
These four lowly pine tips
These four lowly candles,
From your son
From your child,
This humble bit of incense
This humble bit of smoke,
From your sons
From your children.

For this I beseech divine pardon
For this I beg divine forgiveness
That you do not yet lose,
That you do not yet throw away
From your lordly back
From your holy side,
Your sons,
Your children
Who have sickness
Who have pain
Who are suffering
Who are miserable
In one afternoon
In one morning
Who no longer are well
Who no longer are healthy
Who no longer receive
Who no longer possess
The flower of your divine sunbeams,
The flower of your divine shade. . . .

At *Kalvaryo* the ritual sequence described is performed, and then the sacrificial chicken is killed and left for the gods in a small opening on the west side of the mountain. The shaman places the chicken inside with the head pointing east because this is the direction where the sun rises and comes to receive it. Then the curing party has a meal beside the shrine before they start the long march home.

13. Upon arrival at the patient's home, the shaman lights candles at the house cross and burns incense. Then they enter the house, greeting first the table, then the hearth, and finally all the people who remained at home.

14. The shaman washes the patient's hands and feet with the same water that was used for the bath, and the patient climbs through the arch into the platform bed, beautifully decorated with the pine tips and flowers, called a "corral." The shaman

censes the patient and prays to the Ancestors to watch over him. He next kills a second black chicken and tosses it onto the patient. If the chicken jumps vigorously while dying, it means the patient will improve. When dead, the chicken is placed, head to the East, beside the patient's head. It is later hung up on a hook beside the bed, and finally is eaten by the patient.

15. The shaman then proceeds to call the "inner soul," first performing the divination with kernels of maize to determine how many parts are missing. Starting at the house cross, and then moving to other locations where "soul loss" is believed to have occurred, the shaman lights candles, prays, then strikes the ground with a wand of pine and/or oak branches and shouts "Come, come!" while a Mayor blows a shrill whistling sound with a small gourd to attract the attention of the souls. The parts of the soul are finally gathered up and "led" back into the house and into the body of the patient.

16. A final ritual meal is then consumed by the shaman, the Mayores, and the clothes washers, while the patient eats in his bed. The shaman is escorted home by a Mayor who carries the shaman's gifts of liquor, chickens, tortillas, and rolls.

17. For a period of two weeks or more (depending upon the prescription left by the shaman), strong taboos are imposed on the patient: there must always be a woman in the house watching the patient; the patient must stay in bed and cannot talk; no visitor can enter the house, and so on. It is believed that during this period the Ancestors come regularly to visit the patient and see how he is getting along.

18. At the end of the period of seclusion, the shaman is fetched again to remove the flowers from the patient's bed. He rubs the patient with the flowers, which are then sent to be left in the branches of a tree at *Kalvaryo*. The bones and feathers of the chicken that was eaten by the patient are buried in a hole behind the house cross. Then a ritual meal is served.

19. After the flowers are removed, the patient still waits three more days before he can get out of bed. Accompanied by his wife or mother, he takes a series of three sweat baths at three-day intervals. After the first bath, the patient no longer requires his guardian, but may go outside alone. After the second bath, he can go outside and stay there alone. After the third bath, he can go out and his bed need no longer be watched. He gradually resumes his normal activities, and the cure is ended.

The symbolic meanings of this lengthy curing ceremony are rich and complex. Since the patient has been punished by the angry Ancestral Gods who have let his animal spirit companion out of its corral to wander desolately alone in the woods, much of the ritual action focuses upon asking pardon of the gods and providing them with the "meal" of the black chicken, which becomes a sacrificial substitute for the life of the patient. But note that the placing of the patient in a bed, designated explicitly as a "corral" and surrounded by bundles of pinetree tops and flowers, is structurally similar to what the ceremony seeks to accomplish: to round up the animal spirit companion of the patient and place it safely back in its corral (surrounded by pine trees and flowers in the mountains) where it will again be fed and cared for by the Ancestral Gods. At a deeper level of meaning, there is not only a comment here about the relation of wild nature to domesticated culture, but also more specifically about how animal spirit companions are wild animals kept in a corral—just as the wild, unruly impulses of people must be contained by social and cultural rules. In brief, the ceremony serves to re-socialize a person who has become wild and unruly in Zinacanteco society (Vogt 1976).

WITCHCRAFT

The most common form of witchcraft in Zinacantan is *'ak'chamel*, the "throwing of illness." Zinacantecos believe there are two kinds of shamans. One type is "good" and knows only how to cure; the other, called *h'ak'chamel h'ilol* ("thrower of illness shaman"), knows not only how to cure, but also how to give illness to others. These dangerous shamans maintain small cross shrines in hidden caves near their hamlets where they go to perform rituals for "throwing illness." They use small candles of seven different colors, which they cut in half and light upside down, or cut into thirteen pieces and burn, as they say their wicked prayers. The witch can transmit the illness to his victim either by performing a further ritual to "sell" the "inner soul" of the victim to the Earth Owner, or by offering the victim food or liquor that contains "poisonous" substances. As the witch offers the liquor, he smiles and pretends to be a friend, but "in his heart" he is repeating the prayer he said in the cave to harm the victim.

In a second method, the witch transforms himself into an animal, ordinarily a male goat with long horns, and goes about looking for victims at night. A third, and rare, form is for the witch to cut a piece of beef into the form of the victim, stick pins in the head, and bury this symbol of the victim in a cemetery.

The victims of witchcraft are usually men who have accumulated excessive wealth or power, which leads other men in their parajes to become envious of them, especially if the wealthy and powerful man refuses to serve in expensive cargos and thereby expend his excess wealth for communal ceremonies.

There are also three kinds of curing ceremonies performed by Zinacantecos called "on account of witchcraft," which are considered dangerous and evil because their anti-witchcraft procedures may involve turning the illness on to others:

1. In a ceremony called "pardon," small candles of seven different kinds (white, black, red, yellow, green, multicolored, and tallow) are set before the cross shrines. The purpose is to "close the eyes" of the witch who is causing trouble for the patient. This ceremony is borderline between "good" and "bad." When it involves a pilgrimage to Zinacantan Center it can be called "asking pardon" and is therefore classified as a "good" ceremony. But since the small candles (which are also used to "throw illness") are utilized, it has suspicious elements.
2. If the "pardon" ceremony is held entirely at home, it is called "throwing back," meaning that the purpose is to throw the illness back to the witch. In this case, it is unequivocally a "bad" ceremony.
3. "Searching for our inner souls in the earth" involves a pilgrimage to special caves

where the shaman can communicate with the Earth Owner and persuade him to release a soul that has supposedly been sold.

NEW HOUSE CEREMONIES

When a new house is completed in Zinacantan, a chicken must be buried under the center of the house, and a shaman must be called upon to perform a ceremony to compensate the Earth Owner for the wood, palm, and mud that have all been taken from his domain. The essential phases of the ceremony include the lighting of candles and the chanting of appropriate prayers first at the house cross and then at five locations inside the house—the four corners and the center (above the buried chicken).

RAIN-MAKING CEREMONIES

In years of severe drought, certain specialized shamans perform the rain-making ceremony, which requires four days and is the longest ritual performed by shamans. A pilgrimage is made from Zinacantan Center to the precipitous summit of *'its'inal muk'ta vits* ("Junior Great Mountain"), which is considered to be the "younger brother" of the Senior Great Mountain where the "animal spirit companions" are corralled. This Junior Great Mountain is located over 30 miles from Zinacantan Center. The pilgrimage involves guitar, harp, and violin players, two candle carriers, and two shamans, marching in that order. They are accompanied by assistants and two mules loaded with food and ritual materials. It takes over twenty-four hours to reach the summit of the Junior Great Mountain where a shrine is maintained on the west side of a large prehistoric platform mound. Here, facing east, the shamans offer candles, incense, and prayers to the gods who live inside the mountain and are believed to have special control of rains.

YEAR RENEWAL CEREMONIES

The Year Renewal ceremonies are performed twice a year in most hamlets—for the "New Year" and "End of Year"—and three times a year in the Ceremonial Center—"New Year," "Middle of Year," and "End of Year." For the hamlets, the essence of the ceremony, performed by all male shamans who are resident in a hamlet, is a pilgrimage to the Ceremonial Center to offer candles and incense at all the cross shrines at the foot and on top of the sacred mountains around the Center. The ceremony appears to be a symbolic way of relating the outlying hamlets to the tribal ancestral gods in the Center.

For the three Year Renewal ceremonies in the Center, the ritual is performed by the shamans who live in the Center plus two from each hamlet.

The shamans from the hamlets are not of high rank, but rather are the new and more junior members of the group who are sent to the Center and then on the most arduous pilgrimages. The shamans assemble at the house of the Big Alcalde, the highest ranking cargoholder, who is the host for a ritual meal attended by both the shamans and the top members of the cargo hierarchy. Following a complex series of prayers and rituals, the more junior shamans are sent out in pairs to light candles and pray at the more distant mountains, while the most senior shamans, accompanied by the Alcades and Regidores, visit the churches and nearby sacred mountains. The entire assemblage of shamans and cargoholders meet at *Kalvaryo* the following morning; here the shamans pray in unison to the gods at *Kalvaryo* and then, pivoting around counter-clockwise in kneeling position, to all the gods in the sacred mountains around the valley of Zinacantan Center. They then all eat a meal behind the shrine on *Kalvaryo*, afterwards returning to the house of the Big Alcalde for a final ritual meal. The ceremony has deep structural significance for Zinacantan because it links together the two peaks of sacred terrestrial power—the top-ranking cargoholders and the top-ranking shamans—and relates them both to the all-important Ancestral Gods in the supernatural world.

8/Replication in Zinacantan

Over the centuries Zinacantan has evolved a network of beliefs, symbols, structural forms, and behavioral sequences that, taken together, form a consistent way of life. This way of life includes social structural forms and ritual behaviors that are systematically replicated at various levels in Zinacanteco society; it also includes concepts, expressed explicitly in Tzotzil, that are replicated in many different domains of Zinacanteco culture. It is as if the Zinacantecos have constructed a model for their social and ritual behavior and for conceptualization of the natural and cultural world, which functions like a kind of computer that generates rules for appropriate behavior at each level of the society as well as for the appropriate conceptualization of phenomena experienced in different domains of the culture. If the ethnographer working in Zinacantan can arrive at an understanding of the model and the rules that are generated, then he will have decoded the system and will have mastered what he needs to know to behave properly in the myriad of settings and contexts he confronts in Zinacanteco society.

STRUCTURAL REPLICATION

Structural replication occurs in both the social and the ritual system. In the social system the settlement pattern takes the form of an aggregate of aggregates ranging from a single house in a compound to the total *municipio* with its Ceremonial Center, which forms the focal point for tribal activities. Similarly, the social structure consists of units of progressively increasing scale: the domestic group occupying a house compound; the *sna* composed of one or more localized patrilineages; the hamlets; and finally the Ceremonial Center. Not all these social levels are found in every hamlet. In the smaller hamlets the total unit may consist of a single waterhole group; in some of the larger hamlets each *sna* may have its own waterhole, so that *sna* and waterhole group coincide. But in the larger, more differentiated hamlets, the levels in the social structure follow the model provided in Fig. 8-1.

Just as there exists a social order of ascending scale from the domestic group, through the *sna*, the waterhole group, the hamlet, and the municipio, there is also an exactly parallel ceremonial order of ascending scale that expresses the social order both in terms of ritual paraphernalia and in terms

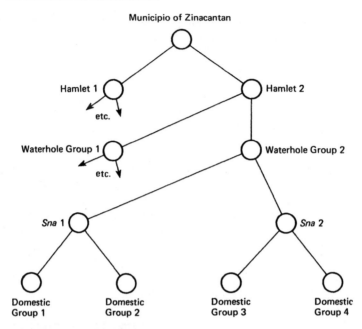

Figure 8-1. Social structural levels in Zinacantan.

of ceremonies of increasing size and complexity. In each case the "nodes," expressed by circles on the diagram, are symbolized by shrines composed of crosses that are conceptualized by the Zinacantecos as "doorways," or, in other words, as means of communication with the supernaturals—the Ancestral Gods and the Earth-Owner.

Within the context of the domestic group in its house compound there are a series of ceremonies that involve only close kin and never require the services of more than one shaman. Typical examples are curing ceremonies for members of the family and new house dedication ceremonies.

For each *sna* there are *K'in Krus* ceremonies performed in May and in October that involve both the services of all the shamans who live in the *sna* and the participation of all of the members of the *sna*. This ceremony appears to be a symbolic way of expressing the rights of the members of the *sna* in the lands they now occupy, rights that have been inherited from their patrilineal ancestors.

For each waterhole group there are also *K'in Krus* ceremonies performed semiannually, typically preceding by a few days in May and in October the *K'in Krus* rituals of the *snas*. Again, all of the shamans living in the waterhole group assemble to perform, and the participation of all the families living in the waterhole group is expected. This ceremony appears to express the rights the members of the waterhole group have to use water from a common waterhole and the obligations they have to care for the waterhole properly.

The hamlet unit is ritually defined by two annual ceremonies performed by all of the shamans living in the hamlet. These ceremonies, called "New Year" and "End of Year," symbolize the unity of the hamlet and its relationship to the tribal ancestral gods in the Ceremonial Center.

The municipio, or tribal unit, is ritually expressed by the complex rituals performed by the cargoholders described in Chapter 7.

As one ascends the scale in this ceremonial order it becomes evident that ritual sequences of behavior performed by a handful of people within the domestic group are replicated in larger contexts with increasing numbers of participants and ever-increasing elaboration. I shall utilize first the ritual meal as one context for ritual behavior that appears to exemplify in its details the general rules for appropriate behavioral sequences in a number of other contexts.

Ordinary meals in Zinacanteco homes are served on the ground in pottery or gourd bowls. The men sit on small chairs and eat their tortillas and beans from containers; the women eat later sitting on the ground near the fire. Whenever there is a ceremonial occasion, a ritual meal *(ve'el ta mesha)* is served, following carefully prescribed etiquette. The most important rules are these:

Rule 1: The meal must be served on a wooden rectangular table. Every Zinacanteco house contains one or more of these small wooden tables. They vary in size from approximately 30 × 45 cm. to 60 × 90 cm. and are approximately 30 cm. high. Some are constructed by the Zinacantecos; more commonly they are purchased from the neighboring Chamulas who specialize in the making of small wooden tables and chairs, which they sell in the market in San Cristobal Las Casas.

Rule 2: The table must always be oriented with the long axis running east-west. The importance of the direction east in other rituals has already been noted (see, for example, Chapter 6 on funerals and Chapter 7 on curing ceremonies).

Rule 3: The table must be covered with a pink and white striped tablecloth. The women weave this cloth on backstrap looms from cotton thread. The same cloth is used to carry candles from San Cristobal for the ritual.

Rule 4: A bottle of rum and a bowl of salt must be placed in the center of the east end of the table. This action designates the east end of the table as the "head" of the table.

Rule 5: The commensalists must sit in small wooden chairs (also made by the Chamulas) at the table in strict rank order. The rank order is expressed in the following diagram:

Rule 6: The meal consists of rum, maize tortillas, chicken cooked in broth with chile, coffee, and small rolls of wheat flour made by Ladinos. Pork or dried fish may be substituted if the family is unable to afford a chicken, but

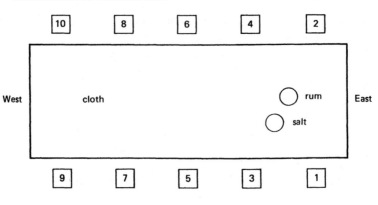

such substitution is always noted and it is clear that chicken is the proper dish to serve.

Rule 7: The eating of the meal must follow a strictly prescribed sequence which consists of eleven basic steps.

1. A young man designated as "drink pourer" serves a round of rum liquor, using a single shot glass for all participants and serving in rank order. There follows the appropriate toasting and bowing and releasing behavior that was described in Chapter 2.
2. The tablecloth is either rolled up to the "head" of the table or both sides are rolled to the middle, and a gourd bowl of warm water is placed on the table for washing hands. The senior man washes his hands and is followed by others in rank order.
3. A gourd bowl of water is passed for rinsing out the mouth. The senior man rinses his mouth, spits out the water, and is followed by the others in rank order. The tablecloth is rolled out again to cover the table.
4. The chicken in the broth is then served in individual pottery bowls and a stack of tortillas in a gourd container is placed on the table by the women. The senior man takes a tortilla, tears off a small piece, dips it into his broth, and eats it. The others follow his lead.
5. The senior man picks up his bowl and begins to drink the chicken broth. The others follow.
6. The senior man takes a piece of chicken, places it in a tortilla, and eats it. The others follow. All of the commensalists finish eating at approximately the same time; they must either eat all of the food served them, or wrap the leftover chicken in a tortilla and take it home with them.
7. The "drink pourer" serves a second round of rum. The sequence of behavior is the same as on the first round.
8. Each commensalist is then served an individual cup of coffee (sweetened with brown sugar) with a roll on top. The senior man begins to drink the coffee and eat the roll. The others follow.
9. The tablecloth is then removed from the table, and the hand rinsing sequence is repeated, initiated by the senior man.
10. The mouth washing sequence is repeated, initiated by the senior man.

11. The "drink pourer" serves a third round of rum. The same sequence of behavior is followed as on the first and second rounds, and the meal is formally over.

The rules of behavior described above apply to ritual meals at all levels in the social system. In the small domestic ceremonies—for example, at curing or new house dedication ceremonies—a very small table is used and as few as four or five people eat at it. The shaman sits in position 1 and is followed by other men, and then women, in rank order.

In the *K'in Krus* ceremonies for the *sna* the table is larger, and more people sit at it. The senior members of the lineage are seated in the most senior positions, then followed by the shamans in rank order, and finally by the "more junior" ritual assistants.

For *K'in Krus* for a waterhole group the scale increases. As many as eight to ten shamans have to be seated at the table, along with the ritual assistants, and often two or more tables have to be placed together to provide a larger surface for the meal. For the "New Year" and "End of Year" ceremonies for an entire hamlet, the scale becomes still larger and as many as fifteen to twenty shamans, plus assistants, are involved.

The maximum scale is reached at the Fiesta of San Sebastián in January, when the entire religious hierarchy of sixty-one cargoholders plus the Presidente and his assistants from the Cabildo sit down to eat at an enormous table and are served not just pieces of chicken but a whole chicken per person.

Whether the ritual meal involves only one family in a small domestic ritual, with a handful of people sitting at a tiny table, or, at the other end of the scale, the religious hierarchy seated in full regalia at an enormous table, consuming entire chickens, the rules of behavior are precisely the same. What is done in the small thatched houses of individual families is replicated in ever increasing scale for the lineage, for the waterhole group, for the hamlet, and for the whole municipio in the Ceremonial Center.

The same type of analysis can be made for many other aspects of ritual life in Zinacantan. For example, in ritual processions there are also a set of basic rules—the marching order is always junior man in front and senior man in the rear, the movement of the procession from one sacred place to the next is always counterclockwise, the circuit always brings them back to the house where the procession was initiated, and so on. Again, these behavioral sequences are followed whether the procession involves only three or four people in a small domestic ceremony, or, at the other end of the scale, the entire religious hierarchy of cargoholders performing rituals in the Ceremonial Center.

These ritual patterns have important symbolic connections with the Zinacanteco view of the world and the relation of their social system to it. The most important Ancestral Gods are believed to live in the East, and it is no accident that the principal sacred mountain lies east of the Ceremonial Center. During a ritual meal these ancestral deities are believed to appear, sit at the head of the table, and partake of the food and liquor served their living descendants. The living descendants are arranged in rank order at the table in such a way that the eldest (and hence those closest to becoming deceased ancestors) are seated closest to the east end of the table, that is, next to the Ancestors. The "more junior" members, presumably with more time still to live, are seated further away. Further, the marching order in processions following the rank order from junior man in front to senior man in the rear reflects the belief that processions (at least, conceptually) always proceed along the path of the sun—hence the senior man is in the rear, closest to the rising sun. Similarly, processions move around circuits counterclockwise, in what is an ancient and general Maya pattern, following the horizontal equivalent on the surface of the earth of the daily path of the sun (Gossen 1974; Vogt 1976).

CONCEPTUAL REPLICATION

The world of the Zinacantecos is also segmented conceptually in systematic ways that are replicated in different domains of Zinacanteco culture. Again, for purposes of explanation, I focus upon one Zinacanteco concept that appears to exemplify in its details the sort of replication of phenomena in various domains I have in mind.

There is a word stem in Tzotzil, -pet, which means "to embrace." The concept of "embracing" occurs in a number of domains in Zinacanteco life: the socialization process in the family, the baptismal ceremonies, the wedding ceremonies, the curing ceremonies, and beliefs about the Ancestral Gods inside the mountains.

Within the Zinacanteco family it is believed that one of the most important duties of the father and mother (called tot and me') is to "embrace" a child and care for it well so that it does not lose its "inner soul," composed of thirteen parts. For if the child loses one or more parts of its soul, it will become ill, and may die.

At the baptismal ceremony a child always has a godfather and godmother (called ch'ultot and ch'ulme', or literally "divine father" and "divine mother"). Their principal duties during the baptismal ceremony are to "embrace" their godchild while this important ritual is taking place. And the most important function of the ceremony from the Zinacantecos' point of view is to fix more permanently in the body the child's soul so that it will not be easily lost.

At the wedding ceremony a ritual specialist called the hpetom ("embracer") is in charge of introducing the bride into her new home—the groom's father's house where she will live during the first years of her marriage. In performing this ritual function, he is believed to "embrace" the bride and groom, or, in other words, to create a new relationship that will last, one in which the bride will not run home to her parents' house because of unhappiness or bad treatment. In performing this duty he goes through a number of ritual sequences, such as taking the bride and groom into the house, removing their outer wedding clothes, giving the new couple lectures on how they should behave in their new marriage, instructing the bride's mother-in-law on how she should take care of her new daughter-in-law, and then leading the bride's relatives into the house and introducing them to the groom's parents.

During curing ceremonies a patient who is believed to have lost parts of his soul calls the shaman *tot*. The ritual *tot* in this case is believed to "embrace" the patient in the process of helping him recover the lost parts of his soul.

Again, the Ancestral Gods living in their houses inside the Senior Great Mountain take good care of the 20,000 "animal spirit companions" of the Zinacantecos. They have their Mayores ("assistants") feed and water them, and they "embrace" them. In other words, the supernatural father and mother are "embracing" the "alter ego children."

However, if a Zinacanteco does something wrong, the Ancestors stop "embracing" his animal spirit; in fact, he may be let out of his corral and left to wander loose and uncared for in the forest. In this event, he may be shot at or otherwise injured, and, if so, his human companion will suffer the same fate.

In a very dramatic symbolic way the connection between the real world of people and the supernatural world of the Ancestral Gods and animal spirits is made clear in one ritual sequence in the largest and most complex curing ceremony. Toward the end of the ceremony the patient is placed on a platform bed surrounded with pine tips, just as the corral of his animal spirit inside the mountain is surrounded by pine trees. As the patient passes through the gateway of his decorated platform bed, called a "corral" in this ceremony, he is like an animal spirit being rounded up and herded through the gate into the supernatural corral inside the Senior Great Mountain. In this instance, what is done inside the mountain is replicated in the curing ceremony, and in both domains a ritual "father" is "embracing" and caring for a patient or his alter ego in the spiritual world.

Thus in the socialization process within the family, in the ritual life of the baptismal, wedding, and curing ceremonies, and in the supernatural world inside the mountain, "fathers" and "mothers" are "embracing" their children. What is conceptualized in one of these domains appears to be replicated in the others, and the result is an amazingly consistent network of symbols.

The same kind of analysis can be made for many other concepts in Zinacantan culture, as a few examples may illustrate. Another important word stem in Tzotzil is -*il*, which means "to see." Thus, for example *h'ilol* (shaman) means "seer." In the Zinacanteco view of the world there was an ancient mythological time when all Zinacantecos could "see" into the mountain where the Ancestral Gods are now living. Now, however, only shamans possess this special ability to "see" the gods and communicate directly with them. Shamans thus provide critical links between living Zinacantecos and the gods for any ceremony requiring communication and exchange of goods and services between people and the Ancestral Gods. Similarly, the largest, most complex curing ceremony (described above) is called *muk'ta 'ilel* ("the Great Vision") to describe the process by which a patient goes on a pilgrimage to the sacred mountains and "sees" the gods with the aid of the shaman.

Another crucial concept throughout Zinacanteco culture is the contrast between *bankilal* and *'its'inal*. In Zinacanteco kinship terminology, these terms mean "older brother" and "younger brother." But they are replicated in many domains of Zinacanteco culture with a much more general meaning. Indeed, they appear as a way of classifying phenomena in almost any domain in the universe: there are older and younger brother mountains, crosses, shamans, drums, waterholes, cargoholders in the religious hierarchy, and so forth. The opposition is even applied to the Christ figure as noted above: the Nativity scene in the Christmas ceremonies contains Joseph and Mary and not one, but *two* small Christ children lying in the manger—*bankilal* and *'its'inal*.

Bankilal and *'its'inal'* certainly appear to serve as symbols expressing some basic contrasts and oppositions in Zinacanteco life, and our best hypothesis is that they give general expression to the contrasts and oppositions found in the principle of age-ranking. The Zinacantecos are a very rank-conscious people and one of their crucial principles of rank is based upon *age*, or more properly, time elapsed since an event occurred in the life of a person or in the transformation of a natural object, such as a mountain. For example, a man of fifty is senior to one of twenty because more time has elapsed since his birth. A shaman who made his ritual debut twenty years ago outranks one who became a shaman last year—even if the latter is older—because more time has elapsed since this important event in the lives of the two shamans. A *Kalvaryo* for a waterhole that was erected a long time in the past outranks a cross shrine that was erected two years ago, because, again, more time has elapsed since it was set up. Similarly, a senior saint in a temple is one that the Zinacantecos have had longer than its junior counterpart.

So when the Zinacantecos say people or mountains or crosses are senior as opposed to junior, or that a certain man or shaman is *"mas bankilal"* ("more older brother") or *"mas 'its'inal"* ("more younger brother"), they are expressing a principle of ranking that is embedded in the flow of time in their universe, rather than merely telling us that one is an "older brother," the other a "younger brother."

Still another crucial concept that is replicated in Zinacantan culture is the relationship of directors, managers, or initiators of ritual or political action to their messengers, assistants, or "errand runners." The general term *totil-me'iletik*, derived from the stem words for "father" and "mother," is applied to the Ancestral Gods inside the sacred mountain as well as to the ritual advisors who advise cargoholders on what to do when they serve in office. In the supernatural world the *totilme'iletik* have their Mayores (assistants) who water and feed the animal spirit companions, and who are sent to summon the "inner soul" of a potential shaman to appear inside the Senior Great Mountain and take an oath to become a shaman. Similarly, in the real world the *Presidente* handles disputes and trouble cases in front of the Cabildo. He is called *totik Presidente*, "father President," and he has his twelve mayores to call upon to run errands, arrest culprits, and so on. Again, in a curing ceremony, the shaman is called *totik*, if male, *me'tik*, if female, and the assistants, provided by the family of the patient, are Mayores to help with the ritual. Similarly, hummingbirds and night-flying moths serve as Mayores for the Ancestral Deities. The hummingbird acts as a messenger and carries out duties like checking on particular families to report back to the *totilme-'iletik* about the state of their health. The *h'ak'chamel ts'unun* (a type of night-f'ying   insect or moth) is sent by witches to announce impending evil to a household.

We have also discovered that names for parts of the human body are replicated in the names for parts of houses and for parts of mountains. In the case of a Zinacanteco house, the walls are called "stomach," the corners are called "ears," and the roof is called the "head." The purpose of the new house dedication ceremony is to provide a soul for the house just as a human body is provided a soul by the Ancestral Gods. The same concepts are applied to mountains: the peak is a "head," the base are the "feet," and the sides of the mountain are called the "stomach." Some of the same terms are applied to fields and tables. The corners of a field are the "ears," as are the corners of a table. The top of a table is a "head" and its legs are its "feet."

More generally, the Zinacantecos appear to conceive of a house, a maize field, a mountain, and the cosmos with directional and spatial symbols that replicate a single quadrilateral model. Perhaps the Zinacanteco sacred mountains—the residences of their Ancestral Gods—are the modern equivalent of the pyramids constructed in ancient Maya ceremonial centers. If the figures carved in stone on the roof-combs of the pyramids and on the stelae erected in front of the pyramids were representations of ancestral deities or rulers who later became ancestral deities, then it is possible that the pyramids had a significance for the ancient Maya similar to that which the sacred mountains have for contemporary Zinacantecos. In this case, the pyramids also replicated the quadrilateral, quincuncial cosmos in which the ancient Maya dwelled and the modern Maya now live.

9/Continuity and Change in Zinacantan

The question I am most frequently asked about Zinacantan concerns the extent to which the contemporary culture contains or reflects Pre-Columbian patterns; or, phrased somewhat differently, what proportion or part of the culture is Ancient Mayan and what proportion is post-Conquest Spanish or Ladino fashioned during the Colonial Period, then transformed in the last century by the forces of the modern world?

Anthropologists have discovered that no culture is totally static and unchanging. The changes may seem painfully slow, as they undoubtedly were in the Paleolithic, or they may proceed at a breakneck pace, as in the contemporary world. But we have also discovered that cultures display remarkable continuities that persist for hundreds or even thousands of years. The most impressive continuities are structural principles that evolved as the members of an ancestral culture coped with the natural environment, faced problems of order and disorder in their society, and wondered about the meaning of life and death and the movements of the sun, moon, and stars.

In other words, a culture is a complicated combination of structural continuities and constant changes, and Zinacantan in the final decade of the twentieth century is no exception, as will be evident as I look briefly at some important domains of Zinacanteco culture and delineate what we have discovered about its continuities and changes. The continuities are most evident in language, cosmology, and ritual life; the major changes have been demographic, technological, and economic.

LANGUAGE AND COSMOLOGY

Perhaps the most impressive continuity in Zinacanteco culture is the persistence of the language. Although increasing numbers of Zinacantecos are learning Spanish, in school or in wagework jobs for Ladinos, all of them speak fluent Tzotzil, and speak it by preference when they are at home in Zinacantan. To be sure, the Tzotzil that is spoken today has an increasing number of loan words from Spanish, but the grammar—which follows important structural principles or rules—and most of the vocabulary are Tzotzil Maya, not Spanish. Further, it is clear from our recent field research that Zinacantecos continue to think and dream in Tzotzil.

The implications of this basic persistence of the Tzotzil language are, of course, profound for their cosmology. The casual observer might think that contemporary schooling combined with radio listening, and some television viewing, would by now have altered significantly the Zinacanteco's view of the universe. But compared to the school learning, consider the intense experiences of Zinacanteco children in the family households, with shamans arriving frequently to perform ceremonies and pray in Tzotzil to the Ancestral Gods, to Holy Father Sun, and Holy Mother Moon, or with their parents on a visit in the Ceremonial Center observing the dancing and the ritual dramas of the cargoholders carrying on their witty dialogues in Tzotzil.

It is not surprising that the Zinacanteco universe with its quadrilateral cosmos, its Ancestors in the mountains, its Earth Owner under the ground, and its Saints, Souls, and Crosses is intact and vital.

FAMILY AND SOCIAL LIFE

The family and social life of Zinacantan manifests considerably more ongoing change. The house compounds are still present, but the houses are rarely constructed of wattle and daub walls and thatched roofs. Instead, adobe (or cement block) walls with tile roofs (or, in some cases, even laminated roofs) have replaced the old style houses in almost all of Zinacantan. The tiles, adobes, and cement blocks are a mixed blessing. While they provide a more permanent house, this type of construction is dangerous during earthquakes that are frequent in southern Mexico. During the devastating earthquake of 1977 in Guatemala, just across the border from the land of the Zinacantecos, most Indians who were killed lived in houses with tile roofs and heavy adobe walls (an architectural style introduced by the Spaniards) that collapsed upon them; the families who still lived in the more traditional wattle and daub houses with thatched roofs were spared.

Since the electrification programs of the Mexican government have reached into every major hamlet, Zinacantecos now proudly turn on their electric lights after dark and play their radios and record players. There are also telephones in some of the larger hamlets, and a few families have purchased television sets.

There are a few multi-roomed houses, but most are still single room structures with the fire in the open hearth on the floor. There has been an increase in the use of factory-manufactured utensils in recent years, including pots and pans, enamel and plastic cups, bowls, and buckets. But the traditional "house cross" is still invariably found in the patio outside the principal house in the compound.

Zinacanteco clothing fashions have changed in style and color, especially in the appearance of much more red thread and elaborately embroidered flower designs in the woven shawls of the women and the *chamarras* of the men. Further, almost all the men now wear long trousers and many go bareheaded; the short pants and traditional hats, hand-woven from palm strips and displaying flowing, multi-colored ribbons, appear mainly on fiesta days in Zinacantan Center or when the men are performing in rituals at home.

Recall (from Chapter 4) that there is a marked trend toward more single biological families living by themselves. This trend is due in large part to the recent experience of young Zinacantecos in wagework away from home where they did not have to depend upon the father for farming land and a plot for a house; and where they could also accumulate money to rapidly pay off the bride price without depending on the father for funds. In increasing numbers young men are also choosing to elope with a young woman, then pay off the bride price with money and ask her parents to pardon them in lieu of going through the traditionally long courtship and complex wedding ceremony (Collier 1989). Fewer extended patrilocal families also mean fewer *snas*, or patrilineages, of the traditional nature we observed a generation ago in Zinacantan.

But since Zinacantecos are returning more to maize farming in the past few years following the bust of the oil boom in southern Mexico, it will be interesting to observe if extended patrilocal families and patrilineages increase again and long courtships and complicated marriage rites become more popular, or whether, as Collier (1989) suggests, the structure of the family and lineage, and of courtship and marriage practices, are irrevocably changing.

Meanwhile, the flow of daily life continues in the domestic group (whether this unit be an extended family or single biological family) with babies being born at home with the aid of a midwife and being nursed and carried on their mothers' backs; with the customary sexual division of labor, emphasis upon age-ranking, and the precedence of males over females in bowing-and-releasing behavior, in seating order and the serving of food and liquor at ceremonial meals, and in marching order along trails and roads—all reflecting ancient, traditional principles of Maya social organization.

THE ECONOMIC SYSTEM

The economic life of Zinacantan has undergone more rapid and profound changes in the past two decades than any other domain of the culture. There has been a burst in population (from 8,000 to an estimated 20,000) as a result of a declining death rate that came with improved sanitary and medical conditions. The consequent scarcity of farming land, the attraction of wagework in the construction projects of the Mexican government, especially highways and hydroelectric dams, and the temporary oil boom in southern Mexico all combined to generate a significant shift from maize farming to other economic activities and to involve the Zinacantecos in the modern world to a greater extent than ever before.

Even traditional maize farming (which continues to be largely of the swidden type) has undergone important changes as Zinacantecos have adopted the use of petrochemicals, especially fertilizers and weed-killers. The fertilizers allow some of the highland plots to be continuously farmed for longer periods; the weed-killers reduce significantly the amount of labor and time needed for the summer weeding operations, and hence permit fewer men to weed more land. This means that the need for large farming groups, composed traditionally of patrilineal kinsmen and/or hired Chamula laborers, has been reduced, with important consequences for the organization of large patrilineages. As described in Chapter 5, enterprising Zinacanteco entrepreneurs who devoted their efforts to growing surplus maize a generation ago are now purchasing trucks and buses and becoming a new type of elite that provides transportation for people and goods (Cancian 1987).

For the Zinacantecos who are not predominantly maize farmers or truck owners, several alternative economic activities have emerged. In agriculture, there is a new emphasis upon flowers and fruits grown on small highland plots in or near the hamlets. Many more men have become primarily merchants, buying and selling the major products of Zinacanteco agriculture—corn, beans, fruit, and flowers—and retailing them in the major urban markets throughout Chiapas (Cancian 1987).

Still others who own no farming land at all have become essentially proletarians who sell their labor. As Cancian describes them, they are of several types, reflecting the diversity of the changing regional economy and the roles of Indians in the system:

> The unskilled laborers work mostly on construction outside Zinacantan. They represent continuity with earlier labor roles, and, as before, they are predominantly young men. The government employees, truck drivers, and artisans (mostly masons) are in new occupations. Most of the government employees work in new reforestation programs; many of the artisans learned their trades during the construction boom in the 1970s; and the truck drivers are part of the expanded Indian role in local transportation that resulted from new roads and subsidized gasoline prices. All of these new occupations are tied to state and/or capitalist development programs that blossomed in the last ten or 15 years (Cancian 1987: 134).

THE ZINACANTECO CARGO SYSTEM

Unlike the rapid, ongoing changes in the economic and social domains, the ritual life of Zinacantan, including both the ceremonies of the cargoholders and the rites of the shamans, has shown little basic change and is amazingly intact.

There have been predictions that the cargo system of Zinacantan would disappear as an important institution (e.g., Cancian 1965), as it has in other Mesoamerican Indian communities, when the rate of population growth outstripped the increase in cargo positions and surplus wealth began to be used in other ways.

As of 1990, the cargo system is intact, with sixty-one positions, and the cargo ceremonies are being performed much as they were twenty years ago. The major changes we note are matters of elaboration or enrichment of the basic patterns (such as the addition of more coins, ribbons, and mirrors on the images of the saints, or the addition of electric singing bird ornaments on the branches of trees surrounding the crèche erected in the church of San Lorenzo for the Christmas season), rather than changes in ritual sequence or structure.

On the other hand, the role of the cargo system in the local social structure has been diminished as the Zinacanteco population has nearly tripled while the number of cargos has remained virtually constant. There was a temporary increase from sixty-one to sixty-five cargos for a few years in the 1980s that came with the addition of four positions from outlying hamlets, but these were dropped in 1987.

With the vast increase in population a smaller proportion of Zinacantecos are participating in the cargo system. This change was reflected in the waiting lists for cargos, which grew longer through the 1960s but became shorter in the late 1970s and early 1980s (Cancian 1986). But, significantly, when the oil-boom ended and Zinacantecos returned home from wagework away, the cargo lists grew longer once more.

The other adjustments to greater population pressure on the cargo system are that rigid adherence to the rules of progress through the four levels of the hierarchy has begun to break down, and three-cargo careers have become an accepted alternative to the traditional four-cargo careers.

But, perhaps the greatest factor diminishing the importance of the cargo system is the large number of civil cargos produced by the state modernization programs. Instead of the traditional cargo service, many Zinacantecos are, for example, now serving as Secretary of the School Committee or as Electric Light Commissioner. Still others find a significant alternative in serving as officers for political parties.

HISTORY AND FUNCTIONS OF THE CARGO SYSTEM

The history and functions of the cargo system as a crucial institution in Mayan society have been the subject of spirited controversy in the past twenty years. The debate rages around three basic questions:

(1) Does the cargo system of the type we observe in Zinacantan have some pre-Columbian roots in Mayan prehistory, and can the system be useful in illuminating the probable sociopolitical organization of the Ancient Maya ceremonial centers? Or was the system introduced by the Spanish Conquerors and/or developed during the Colonial Period? Since the names of the cargos and the saints are entirely derived from Spanish, it is evident that much of the content of the system was indeed introduced after the Conquest. Some scholars maintain that many of the principles of organization have precedents among the Ancient Maya (e.g., Vogt 1983) while others (e.g., Rus and Wasserstrom 1980) argue that the cargo system was a new development during the colonial and modern periods in southern Mexico. Bricker (1989) has recently demonstrated that some of the cargo rituals performed in contem-

porary Chamula have been performed by the Mayas since the Classic Period 1500 years ago. The historian Nancy Farriss concludes that:

> Most of the formal elements of the contemporary cargo system are colonial adaptations of earlier practices. Its underlying rationale, in which prestige and authority are based on material support of the corporate deity-saint, also has deep roots in the Maya past (Farriss 1984: 348)

Recent summaries of the present state of the controversy may be found in Willey (1989) and Vogt (1989).

(2) Does the cargo system serve as a leveling mechanism that helps to erase differentials in wealth within the Maya communities and consequently to contribute to the social integration of the communities? Nash (1958) and Wolf (1959) maintained that the expenditure of funds by cargoholders did indeed serve as a leveling mechanism (like a graduated income tax) and help maintain social equilibrium within the closed corporate communities of the Indians. Cancian (1965) discovered that the Zinacanteco cargo system is ineffectual as a leveling mechanism and does not keep the community homogeneous. He suggests, rather, that service in the cargo system legitimizes the wealth differences and thus prevents disruptive envy. An illuminating review of this controversial point has been provided by Greenberg (1981).

(3) Can cargo systems only be understood by studying them in the larger context of a regional market system and political structure? This question has been addressed by two types of theorists. On the one hand, there is the "dualist" argument that Indian communities are in a separate economic sector that is poorly integrated with the developed capitalist sector. In this separate section the cargo hierarchies maintain a system of reciprocity and redistributive exchange that serves to keep a portion of the surplus from entering the outside market and thus lessens the Indians' dependence on and exploitation by the market (Dow 1974). On the other hand, the "dependence" theorists maintain that the cargo system and its fiesta rituals were essentially a colonial instrument designed to reduce the costs of direct administration and to pump wealth and labor out of Indian communities. This position is argued especially by Harris (1964), who views the effect of fiestas as one of raising consumption standards of the Indians and involving them in commercial transactions with Ladinos who control the commodities they have come to crave. Involvement in the market requires cash, which must be earned by producing and selling a surplus or by seeking the outside wagework. DeWalt (1975), Smith (1977), and Greenberg (1981) provide analyses of this controversy and show how knowledge of contemporary cargo systems of Mexico and Guatemala can be deepened by examining their operations in the context of the economic and political structure of the region and nation. Cancian (1987) and Collier (1989) have clearly shown this to be true in Chiapas with their examinations of the intricate connections between Zinacantan and the regional political economy.

SHAMANISTIC CEREMONIES

The rituals of the shamans are also carried on with great vigor and vitality. A new shelter has been constructed over the top of *Kalvaryo*, where the Ancestral Gods meet on the hill at the edge of Zinacantan Center. But the new shelter is to keep the shamans from getting cold and wet during storms; it has not altered the structure and sequence of their rituals carried on at the old, traditional cross shrine under the new roof.

I estimate that there are now at least 250 shamans in Zinacantan, and they are still actively performing all of the types of ceremonies described in Chapters 4 and 7. On my last hike to the top of the Senior Large Mountain to visit the sacred shrine in the summer of 1987, I met three curing groups with their shamans in a single morning. They were all leading their patients and ritual assistants up the steep trail to reach the ancestral mountain shrine that lies over 2000 feet above the valley of Zinacantan. Each were performing the "Great Vision" ceremony, the longest and most complex of the rituals of the shamans.

To be sure, more modern medicine is reaching the Zinacantecos via the government clinics and hospitals, as well as through the pharmacies of San Cristobal and Tuxtla Gutierrez. And the Zinacantecos have learned to be very pragmatic about trying out these medicines for their ailments. They readily seek dental work for toothaches, casts for broken bones, and aspirin for minor headaches.

But if a Zinacanteco has a lingering illness, or if it is suspected that the trouble may be loss of parts of the soul, or, worse, that one's animal spirit companion has been turned out of its protective corral, or if an enemy is engaged in some type of witchcraft, a shaman is summoned with dispatch to perform divination and a proper curing ceremony.

Further, new houses must be ritually blessed and the Earth Owner properly compensated for the materials used in the construction; maize fields need ceremonies, as do the ancestors of lineages and waterhole groups; rain-making rites are necessary in drought years. And who would think it even possible to dispense with the annual Year Renewal ceremonies that are performed so that the year may pass in happiness and contentment, without sickness or death (Vogt 1976).

POLITICS AND THE LARGER WORLD

As Zinacantan has been enmeshed more deeply into the modern world, the past twenty years have been especially turbulent in the political sphere. Influence has passed from *caciques* ("political bosses") whose power base was control of the distribution of *ejido* land to *caciques* that emerged either from ownership of trucks and buses that now provide the basic transport for Zinacantecos and their goods, or from control of new key economic positions, such as soft drink distributors. Twenty years ago the Presidentes were mainly selected from the ranks of men who held key posts in the Ejido Committees; in recent years they have been truck owners, and the most recent Presidente (as of January 1, 1989) is the Pepsi-Cola distributor.

The fissioning process that has long been evident in Zinacanteco communities also became more evident in the last two decades. Zinacanteco hamlets, especially those located along the Pan American highway, have shown greater tendencies to become more autonomous. These hamlets have created local "agencias" (agencies) with civil officials who sit on benches and settle disputes. If the litigants accept the resolution of the case, then they do not have the extra expense and travel time involved in going to the Presidente in Zinacantan Center. To date, no hamlet has achieved municipio status, but the pressures are there, and one wonders if we are witnessing the kind of fissioning process that must have characterized Maya culture over the centuries as outlying communities flourished in population growth and political power and separated from their parent communities.

The role of factions both within Zinacantan Center and within the hamlets also has become exacerbated in recent years. These factions, often originating in disputes over land, have been present throughout the decades we have observed Zinacantan, but in the early 1980's the major fission became hooked on to national Mexican political parties for the first time. The most dramatic conflict emerged in 1982 when a new Presidente was to be chosen. As Frank Cancian succinctly describes the events:

> The dominant PRI [the *Partido Revolucionario Institucional*] party split into factions that were soon labeled *campesinos* (farmers) and *camioneros* (truckers). In an unusually contested public nomination meeting, the "truckers" succeeded in naming their candidate as the official PRI nominee—which is tantamount to nomination in most parts of Mexico. The "farmers" faction rebelled and voted for the candidate of the very small opposition (PAN, i.e., the *Partido de Acción Nacional*) party, and he was elected. PRI officials blocked his access to the town hall and the records he needed to function as mayor, and official delegations travelled to the state capital to try to resolve the dispute (Cancian 1987).

In this factional dispute the number of "truckers" far exceeded those directly involved in trucking, indicating that the political party affiliation was a label for a preexisting faction. The dispute wrecked the 1983 to 1985 term of office of this Presidente. By the next term, PRI installed its candidate for Presidente, and continued to hold the office in the 1988 election. In spite of the fact that Zinacantecos have very little knowledge of the national programs and ideologies of the two parties, the PRI and PAN labels continue to designate quarreling factions in most Zinacanteco hamlets. And it is clear that this line of fission between "farmers" and "truckers" symbolically represents an opposition between older, more traditional patterns and newer patterns of Zinacanteco life that have come with their increasing involvement with the industrialized world.

Even deeper factional pressures have recently resulted from increasing activity of Protestant missionaries in the Highlands of Chiapas (see Gossen

1989). Most Zinacantecos continue to be Catholics, in the sense that they have been baptized by a Catholic priest, and if you ask them directly about their religion they will tell you they are *Católicos*, even though, as we have seen, their knowledge of Catholic theology and practice may be slight. But in the past decade the first inroads into Zinacantan were made by a Presbyterian missionary who worked for a few years in the hamlet of Nabenchauk. When he was forced to leave the hamlet by the Indian authorities, a number of Zinacanteco families moved with him to a settlement called *Nuevo Zinacantan* located just off the Pan American Highway some 15 miles east of San Cristobal. Here the newly converted Presbyterian Zinacantecos farm plots of land provided them by the mission and attend Sunday church services that are an ingenious combination of their traditional customs and new ritual procedures. As I observed one of these services in 1987, I noted that there was no liquor, incense, or candles—these items being considered either too traditional or too Catholic to be included. But the fresh pine needles were on the floor of the church; the Indian participants as well as the Presbyterian missionary wore traditional Zinacanteco clothes; the prayers to the sick pronounced by members of the congregation kneeling on the pine needles on the floor followed the cadence and style of the prayers of the traditional shamans; and the Protestant hymns, translated into Tzotzil, were sung to the playing of guitars, violins, and trumpets, with tunes taken directly from various Mexican *Ranchera* songs—such as *El Rancho Grande*—which the Zinacantecos have been hearing on their radios for the past 30 years.

Meanwhile, the Catholics have not been idle in the face of this Protestant threat. For the first time Zinacantan has a resident Catholic priest, and he is making every effort to relate significantly to the traditional customs. He is learning Tzotzil, he wears items of Zinacanteco clothing, and he encourages the traditional ritual dances (such as the performance with the "bull" described in Chapter 7) to take place inside the Church of San Lorenzo, even when it competes with the Mass.

WHITHER ZINACANTAN?

At first glance, Zinacantan now seems completely caught up in the modern world: trucks, buses, and cars roar along the Pan American highway and in and out of the ceremonial center on a paved road that has reduced the travel time to the market in San Cristobal from over two hours (on foot carrying maize with a tumpline) to less than 15 minutes by motor vehicle. Corn-grinding mills have replaced the laborious work of grinding the maize for tortillas on *manos* and *metates*. Electric lights and flashlights instead of pine torches illuminate the houses, churches, and streets at night. The scribes, who keep records for the cargoholders of their community-wide collections to pay the expenses of fiestas, now add up the totals with calculators rather than with grains of corn. Tourists arrive, often in tour groups by the busload, and must check in at the *Cabildo* to purchase a permit to visit the churches.

But a longer visit, especially during early morning hours or at night during the times when important annual ceremonies are being performed, soon alters and deepens these first superficial impressions. In the summer of 1987 and the winter of 1988 I returned to Zinacantan, especially to observe the crucial summer (San Lorenzo) and winter (Christmas and San Sebastián) ceremonies. Comparing my recent field notes with my observations of these fiestas thirty years ago, I discovered there had been no changes in either the overall structure or in the sequence of ritual episodes in these ceremonies. Further, the attendance of people from the hamlets was impressive, and the ceremonies were performed with even greater vitality and enthusiasm than in earlier years.

Even more impressive was the general lack of drunkenness in these fiestas compared to earlier decades, when the scene was one of intoxicated Zinacantecos by the hundreds. In the last two large fiestas I attended, with over 5,000 Indians present, I did not encounter more than six heavily intoxicated Zinacantecos. This is an extraordinary development; in fact, it may be one of the few cases in the New World in which a large Native American population has managed to bring the excessive consumption of alcohol under control.

The crucial reason for this change is most probably an improvement in the morale of the Zinacantecos. During the last three decades I have personally witnessed a vast improvement in the morale of the highland Chiapas Indians. When I began field research in Chiapas in the 1950s the economic, political, and social oppression of the Indians was notable, and the consequent morale of the Indian communities was at a low ebb. One index of this morale was the excessive consumption of alcohol in the form of *aguardiente* (the cheap sugar cane rum which is called *posh* in Tzotzil).

In the 1950s the Instituto Nacional Indigenista, founded by Mexico's foremost anthropologist, the late Dr. Alfonso Caso, began to work in the highlands of Chiapas. In subsequent years, other federal and state agencies also began to institute programs to aid oppressed Indian communities. The programs that were introduced included a spectrum of development projects, ranging from improved breeds of chickens to the training of bilingual Indian teachers (called "Cultural Promoters") for schools. There has been much debate in Mexico and elsewhere about the success or failure of these programs. In perspective, it is clear that although many of the programs failed, or were of only limited success, the long-range effect of the Instituto Nacional Indigenista and its successors has been a vast improvement in Indian morale. The important thing is that for the first time in over four hundred years of oppression an *official* agency of the Mexican government appeared, saying "We are here to help Indians." As a result, Indians slowly began to acquire a sense of pride in their own identity; they have also slowly learned during the past thirty years how to be politically effective with government officials, how to borrow money from banks for economic enterprises, and how to purchase trucks and buses (Vogt 1985).

Further, I discovered that for the first time large numbers of Highland Chiapas Indians are living in the principal market town of San Cristobal Las

Casas *as Indians*. In previous decades Indians came to the city, but upon arrival, immediately began the process of "Ladinoization." They learned Spanish as rapidly as possible, changed clothing so as to be dressed like working class Ladinos, and abandoned most of their Indian customs. Now, with the attraction of wagework in San Cristobal, with its burgeoning population, and with the arrival of Indian Protestant converts who have been forced to leave their native communities, the Indians are locating plots of land and building or buying houses and maintaining their Indian clothing styles and many of their customs. The Protestant movement has had the effect of energizing the traditional Maya work ethic: get up early, work hard, and be punctual. One of the results is that the San Cristobal market, which was previously dominated by Ladinos, is slowly coming more and more under the control of Indian merchants and entrepreneurs. While this process has involved the large Chamula population more than it has the Zinacantecos, the latter are beginning to participate as well.

While we used to describe "the Ladinoization of the Indians" as one of the basic processes of change in the Highlands of Chiapas, we are now beginning to consider "the Indianization of San Cristobal" as a crucial contemporary trend.

As Zinacantan approaches the twenty-first century, it presents an overall image of reproductive success, cultural vitality, and a generally successful, if somewhat uneasy, adjustment to the modern world.

Glossary

Affinal Relatives: Relatives by marriage; that is, relatives who are connected with each other by one or more marital links.

Collateral Relatives: Relatives connected to "Ego" (the person speaking) by way of sibling relationships in each generation. They are not in "Ego's" direct genealogical lines, but are, in effect, off to each side. Thus, for example, this includes aunts, uncles, cousins (who are the children of aunts and uncles), nieces, nephews, and so on.

Consanguineal Relatives: Relatives by "blood"; that is, relatives whose connecting link is one of biological or common ancestry.

Dyadic Relationships: Refers to a relationship between two people.

Endogamous Unit: A social unit from within whose boundaries members must always select their spouses.

Exogamous Unit: A social unit from within whose boundaries members must never select their spouses.

Lineal Relatives: Relatives connected to "Ego" by being in his (or her) genealogical lines. Thus, for example, these relatives include grandparents, father, mother, siblings, and children of "Ego."

Matrilocal Residence: A pattern of residence in which the groom leaves his paternal home and lives with his bride, either near or in the house of her parents.

Omaha-type Kinship System: A type of system in which the kinship terms emphasize patrilineal lines of descent.

Patrilineage: A group of kinsmen who trace their relationships to each other through a line of males to a common founding ancestor.

Patrilocal Residence: A pattern of residence in which the bride leaves her maternal home and lives with her husband, either near or in the house of his parents.

Patronymics: Surnames inherited from the father—that is, in the male line of descent.

Quincunx (adjective, **Quincuncial**): "An arrangement of five things with one at each corner and one at the center" (Webster's New International Dictionary).

References

Adams, Robert MC.
1961   "Changing Patterns of Territorial Organization in the Central Highlands of Chiapas, Mexico," *American Antiquity* 26(3):341–360.

Anschuetz, Mary H.
1966   "To Be Born in Zinacantan." Summer Field Report, Harvard Chiapas Project, Harvard University.

Bricker, Victoria R.
1973   *Ritual Humor in Highland Chiapas.* Austin: University of Texas Press.

———

1983   *The Indian Christ, the Indian King: The Historical Substrate of Maya Myth and Legend.* Austin: University of Texas Press.

———

1989   "The Calendrical Meaning of Ritual Among the Maya," *Ethnographic Encounters in Southern Mesoamerica: Essays in Honor of Evon Zartman Vogt, Jr.*, Victoria R. Bricker and Gary H. Gossen, eds., pp. 231–250. Austin: University of Texas Press.

Cancian, Francesca M.
1964   "Interaction Patterns in Zinacanteco Families," *American Sociological Review* 29(4):540–550.

Cancian, Frank
1965   *Economics and Prestige in a Maya Community: A Study of the Religious Cargo System in Zinacantan, Chiapas, Mexico.* Stanford, CA: Stanford University Press.

———

1972   *Change and Uncertainty in a Peasant Economy: The Maya Corn Farmers of Zinacantan.* Stanford, CA: Stanford University Press.

———

1986   *"Las Listas de Espera en el Sistema de Cargos de Zinacantan: Cambios Sociales, Politicos y Economicos* (1952–1980)," *America Indigena* XLVI(3): 477–494.

———

1987   "Proletarianization of Zinacantan, 1960 to 1983," *Household Economies and Their Transformation*, Morgan D. Machlaclan, ed. Lanham, MD: University Press of America.

Colby, Benjamin N.
   1966   *Ethnic Relations in the Chiapas Highlands.* Santa Fe: Museum of New Mexico Press.

Collier, George A.
   1975   *Fields of the Tzotzil: The Ecological Bases of Tradition in Highland Chiapas.* Austin: University of Texas Press.

———
   1989   "Changing Inequality in Zinacantan: The Generations of 1918 and 1942," *Ethnographic Encounters in Southern Mesoamerica*, Victoria R. Bricker and Gary H. Gossen, eds., pp. 111–124. Austin: University of Texas Press.

Collier, Jane F.
   1967   "Zinacanteco Kin Terms." Unpublished ms., Harvard Chiapas Project, Peabody Museum, Harvard University.

———
   1968   *Courtship and Marriage in Zinacanatan.* New Orleans: Middle American Research Institute, Tulane University.

———
   1973   *Law and Social Change in Zinacantan.* Stanford, CA: Stanford University Press.

Dewalt, B.R.
   1975   "Changes in the Cargo Systems of Mesoamerica," *Anthropological Quarterly* 48:87–105.

Dow, James W.
   1974   *Santos y Sobrevivencia: Funciones de la Religion en una Communidad Otomi, Mexico.* Mexico: Instituto Nacional Indigenista.

Early, John D.
   1965   *The Sons of San Lorenzo in Zinacantan.* Ph.D. Dissertation, Department of Social Relations, Harvard University.

Edwards, Carolyn Pope
   1969   "The Funeral Ceremony in Zinacantan." A.B. Honors Thesis, Department of Anthropology, Harvard University.

———
   1989   "The Transition from Infancy to Early Childhood: A Difficult Transition and a Difficult Theory," *Ethnographic Encounters in Southern Mesoamerica*, Victoria R. Bricker and Gary H. Gossen, eds., pp. 167–176. Austin: University of Texas Press.

Fabrega, Horacio, Jr., and Daniel B. Silver
   1973   *Illness and Shamanistic Curing in Zinacantan: An Ethnomedical Analysis.* Stanford, CA: Stanford University Press.

Farriss, Nancy M.
   1984   *Maya Society under Colonial Rule: The Collective Enterprise of Survival.* Princeton: Princeton University Press.

Gossen, Gary H.
1974   *Chamulas in the World of the Sun: Time and Space in a Maya Oral Tradition.*
Cambridge: Harvard University Press.

_____

1989   "Life, Death, and Apotheosis of a Chamula Protestant Leader: Biography
as Social History," *Ethnographic Encounters in Southern Mesoamerica*, Victoria
R. Bricker and Gary H. Gossen, eds., pp. 217–230. Austin: University of Texas
Press.

Greenberg, James B.
1981   "Social Change and Fiesta Systems in Mexican Indian Communities," *Latin
American Digest* 15(2):1–5.

Greenfield, Patricia M., T. Berry Brazelton, and Carla Price Childs
1989   "From Birth to Maturity in Zinacantan: Ontogenesis in Cultural Context,"
Ethnographic Encounters in Southern Mesoamerica, Victoria R. Bricker and
Gary H. Gossen, eds., pp. 177–216. Austin: University of Texas Press.

Harris, Marvin
1964   *Patterns of Race in the Americas.* New York: Walker.

Haviland, John B.
1977   *Gossip, Reputation, and Knowledge in Zinacantan.* Chicago: University of
Chicago Press.

Haviland, John B. and Leslie K. Haviland
1981   "Inside the Fence: The Social Basis of Privacy in Nabenchauk," *Estudios de
Cultural Maya* 14:323–351.

Hunt, Eva
1977   *The Transformation of the Hummingbird: Cultural Roots of a Zinacantecan
Mythical Poem.* Ithaca, NY: Cornell University Press.

Kaufman, Terrence
1976   "Archaeological and Linguistic Correlations in Mayaland and Associated
Areas of Meso-America," *World Archaeology* 8(1):101–118.

Laughlin, Robert M.
1975   *The Great Tzotzil Dictionary of San Lorenzo, Zinacantan.* Washington, D.C.:
Smithsonian Institution.

Levi-Strauss, Claude
1966   *The Savage Mind.* Chicago: University of Chicago Press.

McVicker, Donald E.
1974   "Variations in Protohistoric Settlement Patterns," *American Antiquity* 39:
546–556.

Morley, Sylvanus G., George W. Brainerd, and Robert J. Sharer
1983   *The Ancient Maya* (4th ed.), Stanford, CA: Stanford University Press.

Nash, Manning
1958   "Political Relations in Guatemala," *Social and Economic Studies* 7:65–75.

Price, Richard S.
    1968 "Land Use in a Maya Community," *International Archives of Ethnography*
        51:1–19.

Rosaldo, Michelle Z.
    1967 "Ever-Changing Kinship." Unpublished ms., Harvard Chiapas Project, Pea-
        body Museum, Harvard University.

Rosaldo, Renato I.
    1968 "Metaphors of Hierarchy in a Mayan Ritual," *American Anthropologist*
        70:524–536.

Rus, Jan and Robert Wasserstrom
    1980 "Civil-Religious Hierarchies in Central Chiapas: A Critical Perspective,"
        American Ethnologist 7:466–478.

Smith, Waldemar R.
    1977 *The Fiesta System and Economic Change.* New York: Columbia University
        Press.

Thompson, J. Eric S.
    1934 *Sky Bearers, Colors and Directions in Maya and Mexican Religion.* Wash-
        ington: Carnegie Institution of Washington, publ. 436:209–242.

Turner, Victor W.
    1967 *The Forest of Symbols.* Ithaca, NY: Cornell University Press.

Vogt, Evon Z.
    1969 *Zinacantan: a Maya Community in the Highlands of Chiapas.* Cambridge:
        Harvard University Press.

——————
    1974 ed., *Aerial Photography in Anthropological Field Research.* Cambridge: Har-
        vard University Press.

——————
    1976 *Tortillas for the Gods: A Symbolic Analysis of Zinacanteco Rituals.* Cam-
        bridge: Harvard University Press.

——————
    1978 *Bibliography of the Harvard Chiapas Project: The First Twenty Years, 1957–
        1977.* Cambridge: Peabody Museum, Harvard University.

——————
    1979 "The Harvard Chiapas Project: 1957–1975," *Long-Term Field Research in
        Social Anthropology*, George M. Foster, Thayer Scudder, Elizabeth Colson,
        and Robert V. Kemper, eds., pp. 279–303. New York: Academic Press.

——————
    1983 "Ancient and Contemporary Maya Settlement Patterns: A New Look from
        the Chiapas Highlands," *Prehistoric Settlement Patterns: Essays in Honor of
        Gordon R. Willey*, Evon Z. Vogt and Richard M. Leventhal, eds., pp. 89–114.
        Albuquerque: University of New Mexico Press.

1985   "The Chiapas Writer's Cooperative," *Cultural Survival Quarterly*, 9(3):46–48.

1989   "On the Application of the Phylogenetic Model to the Maya," *The Social Anthropology and Ethnohistory of American Tribes: Essays in Honor of Fred Eggan*, Raymond B. DeMallie and Alfonso Ortiz, eds. Norman: University of Oklahoma Press.

Vogt, Evon Z. and Alberto Ruz L. (eds.)
1964   *Desarollo Cultural de Los Mayas*. Mexico City: Seminario de Cultura Maya, Universidad Nacional Autónoma de Mexico.

Willey, Gordon R.
1989   "Vogt at Harvard," *Ethnographic Encounters in Southern Mesoamerica*, Victoria R. Bricker and Gary H. Gossen, eds., pp. 21–32. Austin: University of Texas Press.

Wolf, Eric R.
1959   *Sons of the Shaking Earth*. Chicago: University of Chicago Press.

Recommended Reading

Breton, Alain, 1984, *Bachajon: Organizacion Socioterritorial de Una Comunidad Tzeltal*. Mexico: Instituto Nacional Indigenista.

One of the best ethnographic descriptions of the social and territorial structure of a Tzeltal community in Chiapas.

Bricker, Victoria Reifler, 1973, *Ritual Humor in Highland Chiapas*. Austin: University of Texas Press.

An excellent ethnographic analysis of the role of ritual humor in social life.

———, 1981, *The Indian Christ, The Indian King: The Historical Substrate of Maya Myth and Ritual*. Austin: University of Texas Press.

A definitive comparative study of Maya rebellions.

Bricker, Victoria R. and Gary H. Gossen (eds.), 1989, *Ethnographic Encounters in Southern Mesoamerica: Essays in Honor of Evon Zartman Vogt, Jr.* Austin: University of Texas Press.

An up-to-date collection of important articles on ethnographic research in the Highlands of Chiapas.

Bunzel, Ruth, 1952, *Chichicastenango: A Guatemalan Village*. Publications of the American Ethnological Society, Vol. 12.

A detailed ethnographic description of this Quiché-speaking municipio near Lake Atitlan in the Midwest Guatemalan Highlands; especially focused on religion and cosmology.

Cancian, Francesca M., 1964, "Interaction Patterns in Zinacanteco Families," *American Sociological Review* 29(4):540–550.

A field study utilizing the interaction categories developed by sociologists specializing in the study of "small groups."

Cancian, Frank, 1969, *Economics and Prestige in a Maya Community: A Study of the Religious Cargo System in Zinacantan, Chiapas, Mexico*. Stanford, CA: Stanford University Press.

A detailed description of the religious hierarchy in Zinacantan, with an analysis of the interrelationships between economic resources and expenditures and the prestige of the cargoholders.

———, 1972, *Change and Uncertainty in a Peasant Economy: The Maya Corn Farmers of Zinacantan*. Stanford, CA: Stanford University Press.

A definitive study of Zinacanteco maize farming and the trends of change in the contemporary scene.

Coe, Michael D., 1987, *The Maya* (4th ed.). New York: Thames and Hudson.

A beautifully illustrated and readable treatment of the Ancient Maya.

Colby, Benjamin N., 1966, *Ethnic Relations in the Chiapas Highlands*. Santa Fe: Museum of New Mexico Press.

A summary and analysis of the bi-cultural (Indian and Ladino) system found in the Highlands of Chiapas.

Collier, George A., 1975, *Fields of the Tzotzil: The Ecological Bases of Tradition in*

Highland Chiapas. Austin: University of Texas Press.
A fundamental study of the relation of culture to ecology in Highland Chiapas.

Collier, Jane F., 1973, *Law and Social Change in Zinacantan*. Stanford, CA: Stanford University Press.
A definitive study of the legal system of Zinacantan and its relationship to the Ladino world.

Gossen, Gary H., 1974, *Chamulas in the World of the Sun: Time and Space in a Maya Oral Tradition*. Cambridge: Harvard University Press.
An excellent analysis of the world view of a Tzotzil community based upon a detailed collection of oral narratives collected in Chamula.

———— (ed.), 1986, *Symbol and Meaning Beyond the Closed Community: Essays in Mesoamerican Ideas*. Austin: University of Texas Press.
A recent stimulating collection of articles on Mesoamerican cosmology and world view.

Guiteras-Holmes, Calixta, 1961, *Perils of the Soul: The World View of A Tzotzil Indian*. New York: Free Press.
A detailed description of the world view of the Tzotzil-speaking community of Chenalho, Chiapas, derived largely from the autobiography of a native of the community.

Haviland, John B., 1977, *Gossip, Reputation, and Knowledge in Zinacantan*. Chicago: University of Chicago Press.
An innovative book on the role of gossip in social life in a Maya community.

Lafarge, Oliver, 1947, *Santa Eulalia: The Religion of a Cuchumetan Indian Town*. Chicago: Chicago University Press.
An ethnographic description of a Kanhobal-speaking community in the Northwest Guatemalan Highlands, with an emphasis upon the religious system.

Laughlin, Robert M., 1975, *The Great Tzotzil Dictionary of San Lorenzo, Zinacantan*. Washington: Smithsonian Institution.
The equivalent of Webster's International Dictionary for the Tzotzil-Maya language spoken in Zinacantan.

Leon-Portilla, Miguel, 1988, *Time and Reality in the Thought of the Maya* (2nd ed.) Norman: University of Oklahoma Press.
A brilliant analysis of the Maya concepts of time.

Miller, Frank C., 1964, "Tzotzil Domestic Groups," *The Journal of the Royal Anthropological Institute of Great Britain and Ireland*, 94.
A description and analysis of the developmental cycle in domestic groups in the Tzotzil-speaking community of Huistan, Chiapas.

Nash, June, 1985, *In the Eyes of the Ancestors: Belief and Behavior in a Mayan Community*. Prospect Heights, IL: Waveland Press.
A readable ethnographic description of a Tzeltal community in the Highlands of Chiapas.

Ochiai, Kazuyasu, 1985, *Cuando Los Santos Vienen Marchando: Rituales Publicos Intercomunitarios Tzotziles*. San Cristobal Las Casas: Universidad Autonoma de Chiapas.
A fine description and analysis of ritual life in the Tzotil community of San Andres Larrainzar.

Redfield, Robert, 1941, *The Folk Culture of Yucatan*. Chicago: University of Chicago Press.   ·
This classic study on the changes from folk to urban culture in Yucatan contains much useful ethnographic data on the Yucatec Maya.

Redfield, Robert, and Alfonso Villa Rojas, 1934, *Chan Kom: A Maya Village*. Chicago: Chicago University Press.
A basic monograph on the social structure and culture of the Yucatec Maya.

Reina, Ruben, 1966, *Law of the Saints: A Pokomam Pueblo and its Community Culture*. Indianapolis, IN: Bobbs-Merrill.
An ethnography of Chinautla, a Pokomam-speaking community in the Eastern Guatemalan Highlands.

Tax, Sol, 1953, *Penny Capitalism: A Guatemalan Indian Economy*. Smithsonian Institution, Institute of Social Anthropology, No. 16.
A detailed monograph on the economic system of Panajachel, a Quiché-speaking community of the shore of Lake Atitlan in the Midwest Guatemalan Highlands.

Tedlock, Barbara, 1982, *Time and the Highland Maya*. Albuquerque: University of New Mexico Press.
A fascinating study of the concepts and time and the role of diviners in the Quiché-Maya community of Momostenango.

Tedlock, Dennis, 1985, *Popul Vuh*. New York: Simon and Schuster.
An excellent recent translation, with extensive commentary, of the great mythological narrative of the Quiché-Maya.

Thompson, J. Eric, 1954, *The Rise and Fall of Maya Civilization*. Norman: University of Oklahoma Press.
A very readable description of the Ancient Maya by one of the foremost archaeological specialists on Mesoamerica.

Vogt, Evon Z. (ed.), 1968, *Ethnology of Middle America*, Vol. 7 of *Handbook of Middle American Indians*, Robert Wauchope, ed. Austin: University of Texas Press.
This handbook contains summary articles on the ethnology of the contemporary Maya.

——, 1969, *Zinacantan: A Maya Community in the Highlands of Chiapas*. Cambridge: Harvard University Press.
A full-length ethnographic description of the economic system, social structure, and religion of Zinacantan.

—— (ed.), 1974, *Aerial Photography in Anthropology Field Research*. Cambridge: Harvard University Press.
Contains articles by archaeologists and ethnologists on the uses of aerial photography in field research in the Maya area.

——, 1976, *Tortillas for the Gods: A Symbolic Analysis of Zinacanteco Rituals*. Cambridge: Harvard University Press.
A detailed description and analysis of Zinacanteco rituals performed by the cargoholders and by the shamans.

Wagley, Charles, 1949, *The Social and Religious Life of a Guatemalan Village*. American Anthropological Association, Memoir 71.
An ethnological account of the social and religious patterns of the Mam-speaking community of Santiago Chimaltenango in the Northwest Guatemalan Highlands.

Watanabe, John M., 1983, "In the World of the Sun: A Cognitive Model of Mayan Cosmology," *Man* 18(4):710–728.
A brilliant article on Mayan cosmology based on field research in Santiago Chimaltenango in the Northwest Guatemalan Highlands.

Willey, Gordon R., 1987, *Essays in Maya Archaeology*. Albuquerque: University of New Mexico Press.
An excellent collection of articles by the doyen of Maya archaeology.